MY SEARCH FOR THE AFTERLIFE

A Trail of Clues

By Sean & Dennis Spalding

authorHOUSE™

1663 LIBERTY DRIVE, SUITE 200
BLOOMINGTON, INDIANA 47403
(800) 839-8640
WWW.AUTHORHOUSE.COM

First published by AuthorHouse 06/09/05

ISBN: 1-4208-5078-4 (e)
ISBN: 1-4208-5077-6 (sc)
ISBN: 1-4208-5076-8 (dj)

Printed in the United States of America
Bloomington, Indiana

This book is printed on acid-free paper.

Dedication

This story is dedicated to my son Sean. Without his help this story could not be told in its entirety. His love and support from the other side is a guiding light for me to follow each day of my life.

Sean
High School Graduation
1986

Table of Contents

Acknowledgements

I want to thank my wife Wanda for her loving support; I don't know how I could have continued with this project without her. Her belief in Sean's messages, as much as her belief in my story, gave me the strength to persevere each day, even when strong criticism on the validity of the events detailed in the following pages stood in my way.

I also thank my son Travis, whose book cover illustration I deeply appreciate, as does his brother Sean, who is looking down on him each day.

In addition to the illustration, Travis's unwavering support has always been there from the start. He listened and never judged the validity of the messages being received from his brother. He knows the controls in this endeavor will eventually be turned over to him after his mother and I have completed our tasks and taken our last breath on Earth.

Another large thank-you goes out to my daughter, Rayshal. You read the story, lived the story, came to a seminar with me, listened to what I had to say and offered your support, criticism and skepticism to the events happening in my life.

I accepted your criticism of my story, and continued honing and editing to help others in the understanding of what I had to say.

As far as your skepticism, however, I took into consideration you're living with your husband...**my strongest critic.**

John, John, John...I thank you for your continued skepticism. It makes me work harder to prove that what I'm experiencing is real. I've told you so many things that have happened. You admit it's difficult to dismiss everything as an overactive imagination on my part, or to suggest I'm arranging numbers to suit my purpose, simply because of the number and validity of the clues involved.

Whatever the reason, I did get you to attend a seminar where you personally witnessed a message being given from my son. You're still not convinced in the workings of the other side; however, the door to your logical and critical thinking has been cracked open just a little, thereby offering some form of hope for you in the future.

I thank many of my co-workers for listening, even though I had them trapped with nowhere else to go. Their added encouragement helped to strengthen my own belief in what I was experiencing.

A special thank-you goes to Marilynn for her valuable time spent sitting and listening to what I had to say. She's become a special messenger in certain events that pertain to my story. I thank her for the input, suggestions and moral support throughout these years.

I owe a special thanks and gratitude to Carlene of *Carlene's Florist* in Warrior, Alabama. Because of you my son enjoys fresh flowers over his grave site twice a year. I thank you from the bottom of my heart for your kindness and generosity in doing this favor for the Spalding family.

It takes a special someone to help an author stretch beyond his innate ability to create a good manuscript into a piece of writing worthy enough to take its place on the bookshelves across the country. To this, my hat goes off to Dean George of AuthorHouse.

We've never met face to face; nevertheless, we've become very close phone friends over the past several months as he professionally dealt with my seemingly unending questions, problems and worries like a child walking through the door on his very first day at school.

This acknowledgement could not be complete without my sincere thank-you to the many mediums and psychics who inspired, helped and continue to be a part of this incredible journey and story; especially, Ms. Suzane Northrop, who'll always be the strongest cosmic link between my son, Sean, and myself.

Finally, I want to thank the many strangers I came in contact with during the final stages of this story. Certain words in conversation would start a process, a process revealing many experiences and happenings in my life regarding the messages I received from the other side. I thank them for listening with an open mind.

I thank you the reader for taking a chance on this book. I hope my story will enlighten and help start a journey of your own to find loved ones who've crossed over into the next phase of a continual journey in life.

Introduction

It's very hard to lose someone you love, especially if that someone is your own child.

I've always expected to precede my children in death; not the other way around. There's no script or how-to instructions for dealing with the emotional issues that follow a tragedy like this. Some families are torn apart because of their inability to deal with the issues involved. Other families grow closer in their time of loss, and try to live every day as if it were their last.

I've been lucky. It's taken many years, but I've been able to work through the grieving process and continue with my purpose in life here on Earth; a purpose I discovered while on this journey.

Nevertheless, it would only take a moment or two for me to sit back and recall the heartaches and emptiness I felt when news of my son's death arrived at my doorstep; it would take only a heartbeat for me to fall back into that deep pit of despair and hopelessness.

I've believed in life after death all of my life. Even though I couldn't find my answers in religion, I did find them in a spiritual form of belief. However, I never took the extra step to fully understand that belief. I just accepted what I felt to be true; that is, until that fateful day in March, 1993.

Years have passed and my knowledge in the realm of spiritual belief has increased tenfold. So has my determination to find my son, if possible, to ensure he's okay and to let him know how much I miss his physical presence here on Earth.

If there truly is **life after death,** then there surly must be a way to communicate with them in one form or another. The most popular method, according to mediums, is with the use of electricity.

Your spirit is nothing more than a form of energy. What better way to get your attention and convey their message than making lights flicker, television sets go on and off, or by manipulating any other device that uses electricity.

My son, on the other hand, has chosen a form of communication quite different. I believe he has, and still is, communicating to me through **numbers.** At times, the number clues have been overwhelming. Even my critics have to agree that something is going on in my life that they can't explain as mere coincidence.

These numbers are not always derived using the same computation method every time; there are some more challenging than others, and require the reader to exercise a little more patience and understanding towards my calculation methods to arrive at my final answer.

Nevertheless, they always come with a **feeling** of being sent from him, because of the way my thought process works and my total awareness of circumstances occurring around me at the time this takes place.

Through the help of these numbers, I'm also given clues and various messages; I follow my inner thoughts and react as directed. My journey into the afterlife is done with the hope of making contact with my son, or other friends and loved ones I've lost throughout the years.

Because of this ongoing journey in my life, I've come away with a new outlook. I look forward to completing and pursuing the lessons I came here to learn, and to also let the whole world know what I've come to realize.

I ask you to sit back and relax, take a breath, and relive my journey into the unknown as I experienced it at the time. Open up your mind, heart and soul, if only for a moment, and try to imagine that one day, this journey could become your own.

- Dennis Spalding

Part One – The Journey Begins

Chapter One
Black Monday

My story begins on a cold Monday morning in Klamath Falls, Oregon. The date is March 15th, 1993. The dark colored phone on the wall in the kitchen is about to ring with news that'll change my life forever...

My mother and I are seated in the living room. She's watching television, while I'm reflecting on the phone conversation with my son Sean the previous Friday. We both have appointments to see our doctors this day. My visit is for diabetes; his concern is for his high blood pressure.

My wife Wanda is at the back of the house cleaning. She'd been nervous and edgy the past few days. The news of a severe windstorm over the weekend in the Miami community where Sean lives gave her an ominous feeling; a formidable hurricane had passed over the same area the previous weekend.

"Why don't you give Sean a call?" she urged the day before.

I had spoken with him on Friday, as well as the previous Monday. I called to see how he had enjoyed his first Miami hurricane – and to assure myself that he was safe. Anyway, I decided not to make the call.

During our phone conversation Monday, he'd mentioned to me how he had spent a lot of time helping neighbors and others in trouble. Because a windstorm isn't comparable to a hurricane, I wasn't as concerned as Wanda.

Sean and I normally talk on the phone at least once or twice a month. He'd just completed a nineteen-month training program with *Motions Industry* of Miami. They had offered him a position following his graduation from the University of Alabama. He'd just received a new company car; an added perk and compliments from his new employer.

The last time we saw Sean was November 9, 1992, in Reno, Nevada, to celebrate his sister Rayshal's 21st birthday. He traveled on a very strict budget at the time. This *self imposed wallet restraint* is a trait he learned from his mother Patricia. She and I had been divorced for almost 22 years.

$$11/9/92 = 11/9 = 1+1+9 = 11 \quad 92 = 9+2 = 11$$
$$11 \ \& \ 11 = 1+1+1+1 = (4) \ 1's = 41 = \textbf{14} \ (reversed)$$

…Everybody is milling around the gate area awaiting his arrival: Wanda; my sister Diane, who flew in from Cleveland, Ohio for the celebration; Rayshal and her boyfriend (also named Sean); his brother Travis, and of course Sean's grandmother...my mother!

It had been almost three years since we last saw him. The plane taxied to the gate and the passengers began to deplane. Sean comes into view as he makes his exit through the jet way door. He's proudly wearing a fancy, black leather jacket; it's opened to expose a light colored t-shirt underneath. He appears more buff than his previous visit. His daily fitness workout routine seems to be paying off big dividends.

In his hand, Sean holds a red rose for each of the ladies. All four women have a big smile on their face. They anxiously watch him make his way through the maze of passengers and visitors to our small welcoming committee.

His appearance is quite dapper and debonair. His wavy, dark brown hair and tan features make him quite the picture. With a gene pool from various nationalities – French, Spanish, Chinese, Irish, English, Scottish, Swedish and a small touch of German, what would you expect? Adding to his charisma, he's also sporting a new pair of contact lenses.

Even though this gene pool makes him quite a ladies man, he's not the conceited type by any stretch of the imagination; quite the contrary, he's very caring and down to earth towards family and friends alike.

I remember the time he left his radio remote car in the upstairs attic bedroom at my mother's house. He was about eleven at the time. My mother went upstairs to get something from the room but did not turn on the light. When she bent down to pick this item up, the antennae on Sean's car penetrates her nostril and lodges in her sinus cavity.

What a sight it was when the medics wheeled my mother out on a stretcher! The antennae was sticking out her nose; luckily, I had snipped off the car attached to it before the paramedics arrived.

Sean, on the other hand, didn't see the humor in it. He stood outside, next to the house, tears streaming down his cheeks as he watched his grandmother being loaded into the ambulance. He blamed himself for bringing the car to his grandma's house in the first place.

At the airport, once the flowers, kisses and hugs have been exchanged and the small talk is over, we finally make our way to the baggage claim area and eventually to the hotel in downtown Reno. We quickly unpack the bags and are heading out the door to see what Reno, Nevada gambling has to offer the Spalding family...that was the last time we saw Sean.

Little did I know when our kitchen phone rang that bleak March day in Oregon four months later that it would change our lives forever...

"Hello," I respond after the fourth ring.

"Dennis? Pat here," says the distinct voice I know quite well. Even though we haven't spoken in some time, her West Indies accent is still apparent after spending the first twenty-three years of her life in Trinidad. Pat and I had met during my nineteen months stationed there as a Marine Corps policeman.

"Pat?" I said surprised. "What's going on?" The wheels in my brain turn with curiosity; I sense this isn't going to be an ordinary phone call.

"I just wanted to tell you Sean is...**dead.**" Her voice holds no emotion.

My eyes begin to well with tears. "Sean is...what?" I scream. "I just talked with him the other day; you've got to be wrong," I challenge.

"The police just left here," she replies. "I'm sorry...but it's true!"

My shouts of disbelief, despair, anger and grief cloud the air; the receiver flies across the room. Wanda comes running out of the back bedroom with a confused look on her face.

"What's wrong?" she asks nervously.

My mother responds hesitantly; she's unable to control the trembling in her hands. "I think something happened to Sean!"

Wanda reaches for the phone on the floor; unsure of what she's about to hear, her hands begin to shake as she puts the receiver to her ear.

She tries to piece together the information Pat is relaying; her eyes dart back and forth as she watches my mother trying her best to console me in the living room. Towards the end of the conversation, her eyes fill with tears as her lips begin to quiver.

Sean had been involved in a single car accident. The impact was so severe they needed the *Jaws of Life* to extricate him from the wreckage. The call bringing us the horrible news ended with a click. Numb, we're all hopelessly left with many unanswered questions.

At this very moment, I feel it isn't right I'm still left on this earth. A piece of my heart is missing...ripped out...and tossed by the wayside.

My mind wanders back to a weekend after his mother and I divorced.

I picked him up one weekend to go to a baseball game in Cleveland, Ohio. He was just a little guy but his mind was sharp.

"Dad, why do you give mom money when you see her?" he asked.

"The money is for support," I told him. "Since I don't live there anymore, it helps to take care of you," I added.

"Well, I think you need the money more than us!" he exclaimed. "Why don't you keep it from now on?"

I couldn't believe what this little guy was saying. My eyes watered and I replied, "I can't do that. But thanks for thinking of me."

My mother tries to break through my reverie. She reminds me of the other children I have to think about. "Why does God let children die before their parents?" I mumble. "It isn't right...it just isn't right!"

7

One of the hardest things for a parent losing a child is telling their sibling (or siblings) that their brother or sister is no longer with them.

Sean's sister Rayshal, three years younger, is living in Renton, Washington at the time. I was forced to convey the bad news over the telephone. I'm unable to hold and comfort her as the message stumbles from my lips.

The worst part, unfortunately, is still to come…Travis. Travis is Sean's thirteen-year old brother. I watch him walk through the front door after school. The expressions on our faces are obvious… something is terribly wrong!

I mention how I need to speak with him in the back bedroom. I follow him down the hallway, slowly, trying to decide how I'll break this devastating news to him. Sean **was** eleven years older than Travis; they **were** the best of buddies.

––––––––––––––––

The aircraft is just lifting off on our flight to Alabama to bury Sean. It's still a mystery to me as I glance out the window to my right. My mind spins like a top with questions and no answers: How a car…**suddenly**…with no explanation, careens off the freeway into a concrete overpass pillar? Why would God take the life of a boy twenty-four years old just starting his career? With all of the million cars on the nation's freeways…why does it have to be him? **Why?**

Warrior, Alabama Thursday 3/18/93

Sean's mother wanted him buried close to her; close to the town where he lived while attending the University. His remains are flown back to Alabama. He'll be buried in the Catholic Church cemetery, at the far end of town, overlooking a small bluff to the northeast.

Burial date 3/18/93 = 3+1+8+9+3 = **24**
Born – 9/24/68
Age – **24**

Our two families sit side by side at the gravesite, awaiting the burial prayers, before Sean's body is lowered to his final resting place. A formal service has just concluded inside the church a few moments before. Friends and relatives are still making their way towards the open grave area.

His burial site is protected with ropes around the perimeter. Chairs for the family members are placed along one side, while Sean's casket, covered in flowers, stands alone along the other side. The reading of scriptures will only take a few minutes. His casket will then be lowered mechanically to the bottom of the grave.

As I look at his coffin, across the open grave, my mind recounts the previous times God had tried to take him away from me.

He was approximately two or three months old at the time. His mother and I were living in a small one-bedroom apartment in Parma, Ohio. During Christmas, Pat and I would place Sean in a small rocker, beneath the tree, so he could enjoy the colorful light show above him.

At night, he would sleep in our bedroom. Three hours after going to bed one night, a loud, crashing sound awoke us from our deep sleep; it felt like the whole apartment was breaking apart at the seams.

The apartment building had three levels. We lived on the third floor next to the manager's unit. Our apartment building had a large leak in the roof. Eventually, this leak turned part of our living room ceiling into a dark, rusty color from the water stains.

The problem had been pointed out to the manager several days earlier; she chose to wait a few more days before taking any action. "We can have somebody in here first thing Monday morning to take care of it," she explains. "It hasn't leaked out yet, so I don't think there should be any problem over the weekend."

*As I stepped around the corner into the living room, I saw half of the ceiling splattered across the floor, along with our Christmas tree and all the decorations. The only thing remaining was the rafters. If this had taken place three hours earlier, Sean would've missed his **first Christmas.***

The next time the *Angel of Death* appeared, Sean was about six or seven months old. I'm working at Cleveland's Hopkins Airport for United Air Lines. I was given a message by my supervisor that I had a phone call from a nervous sounding lady.

"Your wife and baby have been in a car accident," she says, the urgency in her voice apparent.

"What?" I stammered. My mind tried desperately to grasp the gravity of what this lady was saying.

"They're on the way to the hospital; the ambulance just left," she adds.

"I'm sorry, maam, you must have the wrong person," I explained. "My wife doesn't drive."

*"Do you have a little boy named...**Sean?**" The sound of urgency again was apparent in her voice. I was on the road within minutes. Where are the police when you need them?*

As it happened, Pat was out walking Sean in the stroller on the sidewalk in front of our apartment building. The apartment manager was returning from a shopping trip in her car. She turned off the busy five-lane highway in front of the apartments into the driveway between the two apartment buildings.

After noticing Pat and the baby stroller approaching off her right, she stopped the car and motions for her to continue by on the sidewalk. Just as Pat started to take a step forward, a large tractor-trailer, semi-truck rammed into the back of the car.

The driver was half-asleep at the wheel and had failed to notice the back end of the vehicle sticking out in his lane. He tried his best to swerve away to avoid hitting the car; unfortunately, the rear of the trailer smacked the back of the vehicle.

The car lurched forward from the heavy impact. The front bumper caught the stroller, and as it careened forward, pulled it underneath. The stroller and Sean barely miss the right front wheel by inches. Sean landed beneath the undercarriage of the car between both wheels. The momentum of the crash sent the car and stroller approximately one hundred-fifty feet forward.

Pat could only watch in horror as her only son was ripped from her grasp and disappeared beneath the moving vehicle.

A few seconds later, the mangled stroller shot out from the back portion of the car. It settled into a heap at the side of the driveway. Miraculously, Sean was still strapped in place; his body was part of the mass of twisted metal and dirt.

*A nurse, who witnessed the accident and was the lady who called me on the phone, told me she thought **Sean was dead.** His lifeless body barely moved; a faint audible moan gave a small glimmer of hope to Pat sprawled out on the adjoining lawn area in tears and shock.*

When I arrived at the hospital, Sean was on a gurney in the emergency room. He was barely conscious and moaned in pain. The skin had been stripped off one side of his face and halfway up the other side; his arms were also stripped of skin, along with numerous bumps and bruises. The x-rays hadn't been done yet to check for any broken bones or internal injuries.

I reached for his hand; his small fingers wrapped tightly around my index finger...he wouldn't let go. He kept squeezing my finger and whimpering in pain. I felt helpless; I was unable to do anything for this poor baby boy who just wanted the pain to go away. Sean spent the next five to six weeks in the hospital recovering from those injuries.

The third incident took place when he was about eight years old. His appendix burst; according to the doctor, he was lucky to get to the hospital when he did.

Now, as I watch his coffin slowly lowered into the grave, I pick up a handful of dirt and toss it on the coffin. My thoughts know this final resting place is for his body only; a place where his family can visit and remember his life on Earth. **His spirit** – that will remain alive for eternity for all of us who believe in the afterlife.

Pat looks at me with tears in her eyes. "We created a beautiful son together," she whispers, still trying to keep her emotions in check.

We're all invited back to Pat and Rob's house after the funeral for a small reception. It's nice being able to talk with her brother, sisters and mother once again after all these years.

Pat offers me Sean's motorcycle, along with his prize Chevy Camaro. "All I want is his leather jacket," I reply. "That's what I remember him wearing when he got off the plane in Reno."

She smiles at my recollection. "Ah yes, Seanie loved his leathers."

A simple grave stone marker had been selected to represent his time on earth. His name is etched along the top. The bottom inscription represents the date of his birth **9/24/68**, and the date of his death **3/14/93.**

14/24

Chapter Two
Moves and Transfers

Klamath Falls, Oregon, early June, 1995

The moving van pulls in front of our house to begin loading our household goods. I've been aware of this move for six months. The control tower I work at is being turned over to the Department of Defense. My family and I are leaving Klamath Falls for our new home in Washington state in a suburb called Covington.

A little over two years has passed since Sean's accident and death. Our house at 4809 Larry Place holds many memories of his visits that I hate to give up; nevertheless, I feel the move will help get my life, and my family's life, going in the right direction once again.

Little do I know at the time how much importance the number *ninety-five* will play out in our life throughout the upcoming years:

Ninety-five = 9+5 = **14**

Seattle, Washington, summer time 1997

After spending two more years in government service working at the Boeing Field Airport Control Tower, I feel it's time to take advantage of the Government's early retirement program.

I have over twenty years of service and I'm over fifty. I can earn half my salary by just staying home. I submit my paperwork to begin my retirement effective July 3rd, 1997.

The government accepts my retirement request. I quickly apply and resume working as an air traffic controller for a private contract company. These companies are all over the United States and provide service at the old level one, Federal Aviation Administration towers.

I begin my new duties on July 7th, 1997, at the Tacoma Narrows airport in Gig Harbor, Washington. It's during this time I begin to sense a keen awareness to the numbers that begin to take hold of my daily thought process.

7/7/97

7+7 = **14**

9+7= 16   16+14= 30   30=3+0= **3** (March)

97 reversed – 79 (Sean's brother's birth year)

For most of my life I've been uncertain what happens to us after we die. **I believe in life after death; but when and how that transformation takes place seems to be a driving issue within my soul.** I've spent many years in various religions trying to find the answer to this age old question, as well as to what life is really all about.

I was born in 1946, in Cleveland, Ohio. As a small boy growing up in the late forties and early fifties, I began my religious education in the Methodist church. I attended a church in Willoughby, Ohio, through the insistence of my parents, John and Dorothy Spalding, every Sunday at 8:00 a.m. Like most kids, I would've preferred playing baseball or football with my neighborhood friends on a nearby ball field.

From then till now, I've wandered from one religion to the other in search of answers to my innermost questions and thoughts. This religious journey takes me through the belief systems of the Baptist, Lutheran, Independent denominational Churches, and finally ending in the Catholic faith, where I also find a lack of answers.

None of the established religions seem to offer what I'm looking for in my search. I've always believed in a higher power...*or God.* I just felt organized religions add too many man-made stipulations that supposedly represent their dogmas and beliefs.

Honestly, I seriously doubt if God really cares if a Catholic eats meat rather than fish on Friday. Does He really care about the consumption of caffeine?

These questions and thoughts lead me to the New Age section in the local bookstores. I read books on subject material such as: *On Death and Dying, Keys to Theosophy, Reaching to Heaven, Re-incarnation, The Phoenix Fire Mystery, Talking to Heaven, Life Beyond Life, My Life with Edgar Cayce, Seth-Dreams and Projection of Consciousness, The Dreaming Brain, Dynamics of the Psychic World* and many, many more.

Television plays a very important role in providing a few answers to my dilemma. The *"Montel Williams Show"* has a frequent guest star who captures my interest almost immediately. This star is the renowned psychic, *Sylvia Browne.*

I begin to follow her television appearances whenever I can. I read all of her published books. Slowly, I begin to feel a sense of comfort; a comfort in knowing I'm finally on the right trail. This trail will certainly lead to answers I've been searching for most of my life.

The various meditation techniques in Sylvia's books prove worthwhile. I become **more in tune with my inner self.** My awareness seems to increase the more I practice these various techniques.

The use of the techniques, I believe, allow me to experience during a dream state **what I perceive as** a visit from Sean. The following is an actual copy of the dream I recorded immediately upon awakening:

15

3-23-99 Tuesday morning.

I'm standing atop a building of some type with a lot of activity and people. I'm talking with ex-Boeing tower employees who have changed careers (reference Shelly in the military service...etc). Someone yells up into the crowd that Sean is coming (this I believe is Wanda). She's down below in the parking lot awaiting his arrival. I seem to be able to quickly descend the structure with no problems of mobility.

I see Sean in a beat-up automobile that is similar to a broken down Jeep. It's open on all sides. He's in the middle lane of traffic, with a very rough running engine. A car passes by him, off his right side, as he tries to speed away from the intersection when the light turns colors.

The car lunges ahead. He maneuvers into the turning lane, hitting the curb, and makes a sliding turn into the parking lot and screeches to a stop. I make a comment about his driving ability at this time.

The car is running very rough...shaking and vibrating. Music is blaring from the radio and I can't hear him speak. I reach in and disconnect a large wire coming out of the dashboard – too no avail – the music continues to blare.

Sean is sitting in the driver's seat and says: "It isn't going to work that way; it's a lousy loaner car! My car is on the fritz." At that second, he cuts off the motor and it chugs to a stop.

The three of us talk for a brief moment (I can't remember the topic). I remember mentioning about going out of town over the weekend. He asked why we were going to be staying at the place we had reserved.

I ask him, "Where would you stay?"

"The Quality Inn," he replies. "Over there – (he points to the hotel across the street) – because that's the best one in town."

Analysis of the dream

At the time of his death Sean looked normal, except his face – around his mouth and nose – appeared slightly distorted. It reminded me slightly of my brother Jack for a moment, but the feeling quickly passed.

Observation…Sean was injured and killed in an auto accident 3-14-93. His facial features had to be reconstructed partially for the viewing at his funeral service. The car that he was driving in my dream denoted the correlation between the car that was totaled when he was killed – thus the statement, **on the fritz!**

Sean's statement that he would stay at the Quality Inn because it was the best hotel: **Observation**…Sean was always afraid to spend money. This came from his mother's side of the family. During our last phone conversation we talked about health issues and for him to not worry so much about the money.

I told him he needed to get out of town. To take his girlfriend, or go somewhere by himself, and have a good time. He deserved it; especially after all of his hard work to get where he was at the time.

Summary

On Monday, 3/22/99, (the previous day before my dream), I tried Sylvia Browne's **contacting your spirit guide/or loved one** meditation technique. I asked for Sean or any other loved one to come across during this meditative state. Nothing seemed to happen during the meditation process except total relaxation; the message must have arrived late, so Sean thought he would come to visit in my dream state.

Because of the above discussions, I believe the visit was real. Sean was showing me the path. A path I have now chosen to follow in order to acquire the knowledge I'm seeking about life in the next world.

Unfortunately, at this point in my life, do I want answers bad enough to lay out **$1000** for a private reading with Sylvia? I choose to be thrifty and increase my knowledge on my own. I become a member of various local county libraries and bookstores.

Washington State area, October 4th, 1999

The transfer is a promotion. I'm the new manager for the control tower at the airport in Renton, Washington. This airport is closer to my residence in Covington and saves valuable time on the morning commute.

This promotion will work out even better, a few years down the road, when we move to Des Moines, Washington. The house is next door to the Judson Park Retirement Community where Wanda works.

Des Moines, Washington, May 2001

The large, red house overlooks the waters of Puget Sound. It's a short three-minute walk for Wanda to get to work, as well as a short jog for me to the pier overlooking the Des Moines Yacht Club. It's always relaxing watching the sailboats and motorboats make their way into the Sound from the marina; or the fisherman, reeling in their catch, along the pier that extends well out into the water.

Even though my awareness of the many things happening around me increased after the move, I'm still scratching my head and trying to figure out what it all means? Am I just imagining things? Or worse, am I trying to make something out of nothing?

A few of my relatives and friends believe that's exactly what I'm doing. They feel I can juggle numbers to make them represent anything I want. They think I'm seeing what I want to see in order to make a connection with my son. In other words, they think I'm desperate!

On the other hand, I believe the numbers are there for a reason; a reason of which I'm still uncertain. However, given a little time, I know I'll be able to fit the puzzle together and **find my answers.**

Air Traffic Control Tower, Renton, Washington

The more time I spend at this new facility the more I begin to recognize some very interesting observations in regard to **the number fourteen.**

My transfer date was **10/04/99.** I manage **four** controllers. The control tower's main radio frequency for local control is **124.7.** My controller operating initials are Delta Sierra (DS), and their number placement in the alphabet string is **4 and 19.** The speed-dial phone number for the tower Air Traffic Manager is **14.**

In addition to the above, this airport has two instrument departure procedures for the runways involved. These procedures are used by pilots departing under Instrument flight rules and who have a flight plan entered into the Air Traffic Control System;

Runway 15: **fly heading 150 until reaching 1000 feet, then turn left heading 130 and maintain 3000 feet.**
Runway 33: **depart runway 33, turn right heading 350.**

Renton airport is located on a map at: **47 degrees 30 minutes North Latitude.** The official opening time, in Zulu (UTC) hours (Greenwich, England time), during the summer is: **1400.**

This aviation Zulu time (UTC: Universal Time Clock) is used by all pilots, airports, and towers across the country, so everyone operates on the same time without worry to the various time zones across the country.

Finally, the official operating hours of the control tower during the summertime are **fourteen hours per day.**

I'm astounded by my observations. I know in my heart and mind I'm meant to be at this facility. The feeling of Sean is all around; I'm on fertile ground.

I believe this place will assist in my journey in search of knowledge and to prove the existence of an **afterlife.**

Transfer date 10/4/99 = 10+4 = **14**   9+9 = 18   14/18 = 1+4+1+8 = **14**

Manager plus (4) controllers = 1 & 4 = **14**
Renton tower radio frequency 124.7 = 1+2+4+7 = **14**
Operating initials DS = 4 & 19 = 4+1+9 = **14**
Telephone speed dial number = **14**
Instrument Departure Procedure Runway 15 =
1+5+0+1+0+0+0+1+3+0+3+0+0+0 = **14**
Instrument Departure Procedure Runway 33 =
3+3+3+5+0 = **14**
Renton airport is located 47 degrees 30 minutes North Latitude =
4+7+3+0 = **14**
Tower opening time (May-September) 1400 Zulu = **14**
May is the 5th month & September is the 9th month = 5+9 = **14**
Hours of operation during the summer are 14 hours per day = **14**

Chapter Three

From Psychic to Medium: Good bye Sylvia...
Hello John!

February 2002

It's been five months since the tragic event of September 11, 2001. A sign of **changing times** seems to be blowing in the wind. My ears begin echoing periodic ringing. Skeptics will say it's a medical condition. On the other hand, I feel it's the spirit world trying to communicate. Unfortunately, I'm not gifted enough to raise my awareness high enough to understand the words and make contact.

The events of September 11th have put everybody on edge. I'm not the only person trying to get their affairs in order. Many are struggling with their faith, trying to align soul and spirit and reconcile their belief with an afterlife, whatever the belief system might be.

$$9/11/2001 = 9+1+1+2+1 = \mathbf{14}$$

When I look back on September 11th, **the number connection** begins taking a stronger hold of my thought process each day. Something is happening, something for which I still don't have an answer.

One day this month, a co-worker at the tower named Deb mentions the name of a new medium on television. Deb knows from our conversations I'm into Sylvia Browne and her teaching methods in the psychic realm.

She feels this new program, starring another renowned medium, will be right up my alley. The program is called: *"Crossing Over, with John Edward."*

I'm not familiar with the name or program, and because I'm such a loyal follower of Sylvia Browne, I never think to expand my horizons and explore other possibilities. I do, however, make a mental note for future reference.

Des Moines, Washington, one week later
I'm lying in bed, channel surfing before going to sleep. And there it is, stopping me between clicks on the remote: *"Crossing Over, with John Edward."*

I call Wanda into the bedroom, and we watch the show together. I can only sum up our response to the show in one word...**amazing!** One of John's theories is: "there's no such thing as coincidence; everything happens for a reason." This phrase will eventually bring insight and new meaning into my life months down the road.

But it was just the very next day that I realized how powerful his message is. Upon arriving home from work early, I get a **thought message** – checkout the *"Montel Williams Show."* Montel's guest speaker is – *Sylvia Browne.*

As I watch the show, I begin to sense a message being delivered by Sylvia. She knows I'm about to change from her psychic assistance to help from a medium. She's offering a – **plea** – to give her another chance to help in my search for answers to the afterlife.

Unfortunately for her, I can't get the *Crossing Over program* out of my mind. I find myself at a psychic fork in the road. I decide to listen to – **and follow** – the thought messages in my mind, hoping this road is the correct path that will eventually lead me to my son.

Even though most of the clues I receive are subtle, they help change the way my thought process works, and the way I act upon it. The dividends provided by this change in thinking will be more than I can imagine as the days and months pass by.

Wanda and I become faithful watchers of *Crossing Over* from that day forward. I even call and place my name on the subscription list for his John Edward's quarterly magazine *"Bridges."* I'm told when calling my order is placed in time to receive the next quarterly issue due out the first week of April.

The following month was March, and as usual, brings a combination of sorrow and celebration. It marks the anniversary of Sean's death, but is also the birth month of Wanda and my mother.

Over the years, since Sean's death, I've become telephone friends with a florist in Warrior, Alabama. Our family sends flowers to Sean's gravesite twice a year; on his birthday, September 24th, and on the day of his death, March 14th.

Wanda had taken a picture of the florist's building after we ordered flowers for Sean's funeral. The picture showed the proprietor's name and phone number, thus making it very easy to contact them with future requests.

The florist, Carlene, hand carries the flowers to Sean's gravesite each time I place an order; a favor she's happy to do since we live so far away. She's also a friend of Sean's mom, who owns a small yogurt shop, down the street.

March 14th, 2002, nine years after Sean's death

This is always a somber day for myself and the rest of our family. My mind fills hourly with various memories of our life together.

I laugh when I think about the time I took Sean skiing the first time. He's around six or seven years old. I took him to the top of the bunny hill to let him slide down on his own. He made it about halfway down before falling over sideways. It reminds me of the old man, on a tricycle, in the *Rowan and Martin Laugh In program.* One second you're up; next second you're down.

Unfortunately, I had to take him back home to Pat and his step dad Rob, with his right leg wrapped in a full length cast.

23

I also remember the time we took him to the Seattle airport for his flight back to Cleveland. We're all milling around the boarding area when Sean and his sisters come running up to Wanda and I pointing.

"What?" I acknowledge, looking in the direction of the check-in counter.

A man, waiting in line to check-in, had his hand almost buried in the backside of his pants, trying to straighten out his underwear wrinkled within the cheeks of his butt.

"It looks like he's digging for gold!" Sean retorts.

The mental conversations I have with him always end on how much I miss his *physical* presence in my life.

A book that narrows my search

John Edward has written a few books about his life and abilities. It didn't take much reading for him to stimulate my thirst for more knowledge in this area. During one search along the bookshelves, I come across a book titled *"The Afterlife Experiments."*

Written by two university professors, their book reportedly proves the existence of the Afterlife. Working from the University of Arizona, apparently they realized their professional reputations would be on the line once their book and findings were published.

Their experiments involve the use of psychics and mediums, and have to be conducted under the strictest guidelines to maintain their scientific integrity. The psychics and mediums' best interest have to be considered, because both their and the professors' credibility were on the line.

Consequently, the professors decide to use the four best psychic and/or mediums available in this profession. They choose: *John Edward, Suzane Northrop, Laurie Campbell and George Anderson.*

Selecting the participants turns out to be the easy part for the professors, because now they have to overcome the hurdle of convincing these four to participate in the experiments.

Every possible question that can arise from skeptics will have to be checked, re-checked, and triple checked, and then those results would have to be documented before being announced and published in their book.

I find the book fascinating. It helps to visualize the way mediums conduct their work. It was at this point I begin to weigh the benefits of receiving a reading.

A few weeks later while at work, a thought message comes to mind. I open the Arizona professors' book to the back section that lists websites for the various psychics participating in the experiments.

After pulling up the web site, I check the date several times to make sure I'm reading it correctly. The calendar of events shows: **Suzane Northrop** will be in Seattle, Washington, for a seminar on 6/24/02.

Within seconds, I'm on the phone ordering a set of tickets for Wanda and myself. The time drags for the rest of the day; I'm anxious to get home and tell her the unexpected **good news!**

$$6/24/02 = 6+2+4+2 = \mathbf{14}$$

Des Moines, Washington, later that day.

I spend most of the night wondering about the upcoming seminar: Should we get there early? Should we sit in the front row to make eye contact? What will be the best way to ensure a reading, and possibly make a connection with my son?

Each time we've watched the television program, *"Crossing Over with John Edward,"* it's been televised from his New York City studio. The format consists of: readings with his studio audience, or the gallery.

At various times, other readings would consist of one-on-one or small group sessions, as well as an occasional pre-recorded phone reading. Wanda and I had never seen anything involving a seminar.

Renton tower the following day

I go down to the break room below the tower cab after the next controller arrives at work. The clock on the wall reads 11:00 a.m.

"Deb says she watches John around this time," I think aloud.

Within seconds, the television is tuned to *"Crossing Over."* John Edward begins the show in his usual way. He informs the television listening audience what they will witness over the next half hour.

Upon hearing the next words out of his mouth, I sit upright in the chair; my jaw drops, and I stare at the television transfixed.

"Today, I'll be showing you something different," he explains. "I'll take you back to a seminar I did in Salt Lake City, Utah. I'll try to show you what a seminar is all about. It doesn't matter where you're sitting; if you're meant to get a message…you'll get a message."

By the time the show was over, every question I thought about the night before is answered. I begin to sense something is going on for which I have no explanation.

My questions are answered

Thoughts of Friends Passed

My awareness of things happening around me is getting stronger with each passing day. Previously, little things would pass right over my head.

I eagerly anticipate the upcoming seminar. I create a list of relatives, friends, and acquaintances that have passed away over the years, as far back as memory will permit. I also search through our old photo album and scrapbooks for pictures to include by their names.

At least once a week, I retrieve my list of names, along with their photographs, and take a few minutes to reflect on that person's life. I think about any time we spent together, as well as the meaning or impact that person made on my life. These meditation sessions always end with a small silent prayer and a thank-you.

This process is done in the hopes of increasing their energy strength; at the same time, I want to create a **mental energy bridge** from my world to theirs.

If any family member or friends choose to come through at the seminar, their energy will be strong enough to allow their message to be received by the medium, and then passed along to Wanda or myself.

In addition, if any messages are received from friends and relatives, trying to contact their own family members who still reside in the physical world, then Wanda or myself will then become a messenger. We will make sure the process is honored, despite any awkwardness in the situation, especially if we're speaking to a skeptic on the other end of the phone.

Her sister's letter floats to the floor

During a confused time in my life, I met a special lady and friend, who helped me get my life back in order after a divorce. She's quick to hire me at her place of employment in a private contract tower, after I had foolishly tossed my government career in the air traffic control industry by the wayside.

By using her friends and contacts she'd made during her lifetime on this earth, she's instrumental in helping me re-establish my career. I move out to the west coast six months later, to begin working for the FAA once again.

Nevertheless, we continue to stay in close contact. Every Christmas ensures an exchange of cards containing lots of information updating each other on the progress in our lives.

One day in January, many, many years later, I receive a letter from her sister informing me that my wonderful friend Lib had passed away. She'd been fighting an illness for months, and passed away earlier that month.

Because I didn't have an actual picture of Lib, except in the scrapbook of my mind, I wanted this letter to be attached to her name, on my list of family and friends, so I can reflect upon it during my meditation prayers.

For the life of me, I can't find it anywhere! I rip through the office files at home on numerous occasions, without success. Finally, I concede that it got lost in our move from Covington to Des Moines.

One week later, while downstairs rearranging boxes in the computer room, a piece of paper flies out of a box and falls gently to the floor. I reach down to pick it up and toss it in the wastepaper basket, when I feel a strong sensation in my body and stop. I look at the paper in my hand, and... ***it's the letter***...the letter I'd been searching for.

Her name echoes in my ear.

During one of my meditation sessions, I can't remember the name of our neighbor's daughter in Klamath Falls, who lost her life in a gun accident at her boyfriend's house one day after school.

I concentrate hard on the words: **newspaper lady's daughter!**

Her name echoes aloud in my ear. I stop, smile and thank Lori Depue for her help.

After hearing her name, my mind wanders back to Klamath Falls, Oregon. I remember how long it took for me to confront her mother, Coleen, after her daughter's death. Having lost a child myself, I wanted to give her all the space she needed.

If I was outside working in the yard and I saw her coming around the street corner to deliver the newspaper, I'd slip into the house, or the backyard, until she'd left our street.

One day, I look up and see her walking slowly down the street with papers in hand. I sense the timing is right; I meet her halfway down the driveway. My embrace said it all. We didn't have to exchange any words for several minutes.

Chapter Four
Lost & Found

June, 2002. (Three weeks before medium Suzane Northrop's seminar)

Wanda and I are anxious for the upcoming seminar. My brother Jack just passed away a few weeks ago in May at a wedding reception for our nephew. After dancing with our sister Bonnie, he walked slowly off the dance floor to sit and take a rest. Within seconds, he keels over with a massive heart attack.

My brother Greg and Jack's son, John David, begin CPR until the medics arrive, but Jack never regains consciousness. He's only 59. I know Sean is already there to greet his uncle as he crosses to the other side.

Wanda and I fly back to Cleveland to attend the funeral. I give a short eulogy entitled, *"Memories of my brother Jack."* At least I think it was short. I wrote the eulogy a few days prior to our arrival. The eulogy included pictures of his life, as well as memory clips of our life together throughout the years. I planned to present the album booklet to his daughter Rebecca, and John David after my reading.

I'm impressed by the number of people my brother's life impacted. I stand in front of a very large group of mourners as I begin my story. I need to reveal my true brother – the generic funeral parlor prayers and somberly spoken memories of Jack didn't honor him with a true memorial.

I feel the eulogy is short enough to say what I have to say in order to convey my message; unbeknownst to me, it lasts over forty-five minutes – much to the chagrin of the funeral staff – but apparently was thoroughly enjoyed by those in attendance.

The funeral staff must've been expecting something short and too the point, so their front doors can be closed by 9:30 p.m. as scheduled. Because I exceeded what they thought was my allowable time, they didn't permit anyone else to come forward and say a few words in remembrance—even John David and Rebecca.

Anyway, I said what I had to say, and I hope Jack enjoyed it. I know our Uncle Bill did; in fact, he told me so as I walked past him, on my way back to my chair. He also requested I write his eulogy when his time comes.

I know a medium like Suzane has no control over **who** comes through with a message, and to **whom** that message is directed. Nevertheless, even though it has only been a short time, I'm hoping a message will come through from Jack, just in case Sean isn't able to make a connection on this particular Monday night.

A message from him will mean so much to his children. It can possibly help get the two of them, as well as their two stepsisters from a different marriage, back on the right track towards healing and closure.

Jack's age 59 = 5+9 = **14**

Tuesday morning, June 18, 2002 (Six days before the seminar)
I'm at work in the tower, and receive a **thought message** to go to Suzane's web site. I notice she'll be arriving early in the Seattle area in order to appear on a television program, as well as several radio stations. I make a mental note.

My thinking at the time is to tape her radio broadcast and television appearance, so Wanda can see how this lady conducts her readings; it also will provide a better understanding of the process for Monday night's seminar.

These special appearances are to take place during the workday, when Wanda wouldn't be able to watch and listen.

Thursday morning, June 20, 2002 (Four days before the seminar)

I begin my duties in the tower at 7:00 a.m. The broadcast is at 8:00 a.m. I have the recording tape already in place; the radio dial is set to the unfamiliar channel. "Suzane Northrop will be on the air with us in approximately ten minutes," says the station's radio host.

I'm caught off guard by the following announcement: **"If you'd like to talk to Suzane about one of your past loved ones, please call the following number......."**

My heart pounds as my fingers react instantly to this unexpected message; the phone rings just as fast!

"Do you have a past loved one you wish to talk to Suzane about?" the voice on the other end asks.

"Yes!" I answer, still trying to grasp what's about to take place. "Do you want a name?" I offer.

"No," he replies. "Just wait on the line until Suzane gets to you."

His instructions echo in my ear. I nervously await my turn; I can hear the live broadcast over the phone. Suzane is connecting another caller with a loved one who has crossed over.

I begin to issue control instructions to the aircraft early. I'm trying to watch every airplane under my control before my turn on the show; I hope for a four to five minute window of radio silence in the tower, so I can give Suzane my complete attention.

I've been on hold for approximately 25 minutes. The pressure builds! I hear the disc jockey announce my name over the air on the radio, as well as through the phone receiver.

Suzane also repeats my name. "Good morning, Dennis, who do you want to talk to this morning?" she asks.

"My son," I reply. "Do you want his name?

31

"No," she responds. "I don't need anything else." There's a slight pause before she continues. "Is this your only son?" she asks. I hear a small hesitation in her voice.

I hesitate for a moment before answering. I explain about a son from another marriage.

She chuckles for a moment. She then explains how my son is also laughing; he's telling her that he's the favorite!

"He's also telling me he's totally different in character than your other son," she relates.

"Can you tell me how he died?" I ask.

"I feel he died because of an accident," she replies. "I'm also seeing a lot of...**smoke.** Not smoke like in a bar; a different type of smoke."

Her reading continues. "His crossing is fast...very fast! It's like...BOOM! I'm here, and then I'm there!"

I listen intently...each validation is right on target.

"He's telling me he was alone when he crossed, but he wasn't alone. Does this make any sense to you?" she asks.

"Yes," I reply. I think back to the accident scene described to me: A single car leaves the freeway at a high rate of speed. It then crashes into a highway overpass concrete pillar. Sean is alone in the car; however, rescue workers and bystanders crowd around him.

"But he's also telling me you've got some missed information. This is coming through...loud and clear!" she warns. "It's like you don't have all...**the pieces to the puzzle.**"

My mind recalls certain family members and friends speculating it could've been **suicide.**

"I agree," I say. "I don't have all the pieces. That's why I'm calling."

Suicide...impossible! Why spend four years working your way through college, successfully land a good career with a stable company, and then throw it all away. Knowing Sean's character, I knew that didn't make any sense.

After college, he spends another year and a half in the company's training program. Why throw it away over a senseless fight or argument with your girlfriend?

*Besides, if he **had** a fight with his girlfriend that night, and he wanted to end it all, then why would he be heading back in the direction of her apartment when he got killed?*

The disc jockey interrupts the phone conversation at this point. He wants to get in a few more callers during the allotted time slot.

I hang up the phone. My hands are shaking; my mind spins like a top. I can't believe how accurate **most** of her validations had been.

When the next controller arrives at the tower, I take a few hours of vacation time and go home; the connection with Sean has made it impossible to continue trying to separate airplanes.

Suzane connects with my son!

Des Moines, Friday, June 21, 2002 (three days before the seminar)

I walk outside to get the mail around four o'clock. Besides the normal bills and junk mail, I see a large, oversized envelope. The return address in the upper left hand corner references: *Bridges, John Edward's newsletter.* A quick thought enters my head. Subconsciously, I quicken my pace; I'm anxious to read **my first issue.**

I sit down in the chair facing the living room window where I have a partial view of Puget Sound. The magazine on my lap, I fumble to put on my glasses.

I quickly notice a headline on the cover, under the heading of *"Points of Interest."* One item in particular stands out: the name **Suzane Northrop.**

Inside the magazine is an article about her, aptly titled, *"Have Medium Will Travel."*

The article is very informative. Nevertheless, I begin to ponder over why this newsletter would arrive **(3)** days before her seminar?

Gazing out the window, I watch large cumulus clouds expanding upward to great heights, slowly being pushed across the sky to the northeast; all the while, thoughts are still cascading through my mind.

"Is this intentional for this newsletter to arrive two months late?" I think aloud. "Maybe, just maybe, we're...meant to go...to the seminar on Monday."

Standing up, I place the newsletter on the table for Wanda to read later and start to walk away when something catches my eye. The newsletter is written for the first quarter of the year, January-March 2002, but it's the information below the publication dates that make me stop and stare...**Volume 4 Issue #1.**

Little did I know the weekend held one additional faint clue. To uncover it, Wanda and I will have to be on top of the **awareness game** being played out before us.

Article on Suzane Northrop's Seminars
Volume 4 Issue # 1 = 4 & 1 = **14**

Des Moines, Sunday night, June 23, 2002 (One day before the seminar)

As we normally are on Sunday night, Wanda and I are seated in the living room watching John Edward. During a commercial, I bring up the topic of the seminar tomorrow night.

"If we happen to receive any messages, from friends or family, it'll be **our duty** to pass it along," I say. "Not everyone believes this stuff is real! It'll be hard and awkward, but I feel the process **has to be honored.**"

Wanda smiles and nods her head in agreement. Silently, she knows I'll be the one making the phone calls or personal contact; nevertheless, I know she'll be right there to back up our position on this subject.

John Edward closes his program this night with the usual: "Love, Appreciate and Validate those in your life now..." It's the final closing clip that catches our ear: "If you receive a message from a friend, acquaintance, or family member," he begins, "I feel it's your duty to honor the process to ensure this message gets to their loved one, no matter how hard or awkward it may be."

It's your duty to pass on messages from friends... **and acquaintances**

Seattle, Washington, Monday night, June 24, 2002 (Day of the conference)

We arrive at the conference location, the Red Lion hotel, a few hours early. This gives us time to enjoy a nice, leisurely dinner and discuss the possibilities of what might happen later in the evening.

About two hundred people gather for the event. Everyone has a pencil and paper; they're ready to write down any information that comes across from a loved one, via Suzane, in her role as a go-between connection to the spirit world.

Suzane stands before the audience and explains the process of being a medium. She relates part of her story from childhood to the present. A few demonstrations are given to emphasize our gift of free will. This gift is given to everyone, from God, or whatever a person calls the higher power above.

During the question and answer portion of the seminar, I recall her article in John Edward's magazine. I feel if I capture her attention, in one way or another, it might benefit in receiving a reading.

"Are you still carrying around the fireman with you?" I ask. "If so, does he have his own room in your house yet?"

Suzane looks in my direction perplexed, a quizzical look on her face. A second later, a smile creeps across her lips.

"How'd you know about that?" she questions.

"I've got my sources when it comes to you," I reply, not revealing the source of my information.

She takes the next several minutes to explain to audience members the answer to my question.

It so happens, after 9/11 at one of her seminars on the East Coast, she tapped into the energy source of a fireman who lost his life on that horrible day. Nobody in the audience that evening could validate anything about him.

In fact, he'd been showing up at quite a few seminars throughout the year, looking for his loved ones. In her article, Suzane commented about making room in her house for the fireman, if she can't find his family pretty soon.

The readings are over before we know it. Only those people who are meant to have a reading **got a reading!**

Even though we knew from watching John Edward over the past several months this could happen, Wanda and I we're both a little disappointed that no family members or friends chose to attend this night.

"We still have the phone reading on tape from Thursday," I offer encouragingly, as we head for the book signing line at the back of the room.

I can tell from Wanda's expression, she'd been hoping somebody else might have come through.

Before I came into Wanda's life during the early part of 1978, she had a special friend – Chris Warner. He was a private pilot who flew out of the Olympia, Washington airport.

This is the same airport the FAA re-assigned me to in November 1977, when I was re-hired by the government. I left Cleveland by car in early November for the three-day drive to Olympia. I reported for work at the tower four days later.

During the 1976 Thanksgiving holiday, Chris departed the airport on a Monday morning in a single engine Piper class aircraft for a long holiday visit with his family in western Montana.

Chris never made it back to Olympia. His aircraft's wreckage was strewn over rugged terrain three to five miles east of the Sand Point, Idaho airport. His body was recovered five days later when a bear hunter came across the crash site.

Wanda felt bad she didn't include Chris in her Thanksgiving plans that year. He held a very special place in her heart then, and he still does. He's also in my thoughts during my meditation times.

I always ask him to take the time and stop by for a visit with his special friend.

Olympia Airport...November...Thanksgiving...Wanda... Pilot/ Controller

Before retiring to bed this night, I thank our loved ones and friends in my prayers for the opportunity of being there with them, even though we're unable to make a connection. I guess some spirits are stronger and more forceful than others. For some reason, the date of the seminar is on my mind as I slowly drift off to sleep.

$$6/24/02 = 6+2+4+2 = \mathbf{14}$$

The next day I try to perform my normal routine, but I find it hard to concentrate. I look over the notes I'd written down from the **phone reading** with Suzane the previous week. When I listen to the tape reading again, it sends chills and shivers over my body; the hairs on my neck stand on end. Every item mentioned seems to be right on target, except for the reference to **the fishing pole.** I still can't validate this particular detail, unless it's a **ski pole** she's actually seeing in her mind?

Replaying the tape one more time, I glance down at my notes. Suddenly **the numbers** I'd written down from the phone reading literally jump off the paper at me!

Less than a minute later the message sinks in. I can't believe what I see. My stomach feels like it's eaten a path to my back bone; the hairs along my arm and neck are once again standing straight up.

On Thursday, I'd written down the **exact time** the phone reading took place; the time Suzane came on air and asked, "Who do you want to connect with?"

The reading took place at: 8:36 a.m. / or 24 minutes to 9. I wrote the formula on a sheet of paper like this: 8:36/24-9. Sean was born 9/24/68. He died 3/14/93. Every number is there except...**14**...so I thought.

8:36/24-9 = **9/24/68** and **3/ /93**

Chapter Five

Contact From The Other Side

Des Moines, the middle of August 2002

A few months have gone by since the seminar with Suzane. My brother **Greg** and his family come out to the West Coast for a visit. I play the tape of my phone reading for him and the rest of his family. I also show him my time and date formula.

"I've got everything except for the day Sean died," I explain.

My brother sits quietly in the chair, looking at the piece of paper I handed him. I notice he's penciling in entries on the paper.

After a few minutes, he looks up with a shitty grin on his face. "Wait a minute!" he exclaims, moving his chair closer in my direction.

"What?" I ask, my voice eager with anticipation.

Greg places the paper on my lap. "Look at the way you have the numbers written down," he says. His finger points towards the original time frames I'd written down. "The number fourteen…**is there!**"

I look down at the piece of paper. I study his computations for a moment; I can see how the numbers fit together. I can't understand how I missed a clue like that, especially at this time in my life with my keen awareness of everything happening around me.

This is the computation I see:

$$8{:}36 = 8+36 = 44$$
$$24\text{-}9 = 15 = \underline{15}$$
$$59 = 5+9 = \mathbf{14}$$

About a week or so has passed since my brother and his family left our home in Washington to continue their cross country automobile trip home to Chicago via California, Las Vegas, Grand Canyon and Branson, Missouri. It must be nice to be on vacation, although I would've flown.

Once again, Wanda and I are watching: *"Crossing Over, with John Edward."* A thought comes to mind during a commercial break.

"I wish I would've asked Suzane if she knew the **special number** Sean and I have," I remark, looking over at her on the sofa.

"Yes," she agrees. "That would've been good."

"Do you remember what it is?" I ask coyly.

"Yes," she responds confidently.

"Okay," I challenge. "What is it?"

"Twenty-nine!" she states. "The number you and he played at the roulette table."

My thoughts swirl back in time…

…We're in Reno for Rayshal's twenty-first birthday. Sean and I decide to leave the group and hit a few casinos on our own. We decide to try the El Dorado first. We share a laugh or two, walking down the sidewalk, remembering the episode at the Comedy Club the previous night:

He always wore dark shades because of the glare on his contacts. The lady comedienne on stage decides to use this against him in her routine of picking out audience members to rag on. Sean tries his best to prevail against her attack. I can see his ego starting to bruise; his defenses are beginning to shift. I'm just about to interject, "Do you always pick on the blind this way?"

I would've gotten out of my seat and escorted him out of the room, but unfortunately she aims her verbal attack on another audience member before I utter a word.

Once inside the casino, Sean and I take a seat around the roulette table. After several minutes of playing, he notices I'm continually playing number 29!

In fact, most of the other participants around the table decide to mimic my strategy; soon the chips are stacked up in a wobbly pile. Before the croupier drops the ball on the wheel, Sean decides to help me out.

"You need to protect that number, Dad," he insists. "Think of it as your castle. You need to build a moat around it for safety. Put extra chips on the surrounding numbers; that way you're protecting your investment!" he adds.

The chips are added, as directed, before the already spinning ball drops into the slot. A few seconds later, the sound of clink, clink, kerplunk is heard; the croupier shouts out: "29!" The table erupts with excitement.

My mind fast-forwards to the present. Not more than seven seconds had passed since I asked Wanda the question. A commercial comes on television promoting some product we've never seen before. In fact, we've never seen it since!

In big letters, filling the entire screen of our large television set, are the numbers **$29.95**. The number represents the **29** in roulette, as well as, the intriguing number…**fourteen.**

"Did you see that?" I ask Wanda. My eyes bounce back and forth excitedly between Wanda and the television.

She can only nod her head in agreement. We both realize Sean is in the room listening to our conversation. What a sensational way to make your presence known.

"Thanks, son," I say aloud. "It's nice to know you're around listening to us."

The next few weeks are spent reviewing notes and clues I've gathered together. Even though my family and I have been fortunate enough to have a taped message from our son through the efforts of a well known medium, I can't help but feel there's still more to this mystery further down the road in my life cycle.

I know Suzane Northrop has a message board on her website. Her *faithful followers* use this resource to exchange different views and perspectives on various questions posed by each contributor. A wide range of views can be quickly obtained on any subject matter with which one chooses to write. None of the posted material is either supported or rejected by Suzane; each person has a right to their own personal opinion on any subject being discussed.

I think it'll be a good idea to share a few of my number theories with this group. The web site questions usually deal with the spirit world or afterlife in general. It's easier knowing the audience has open minds and hearts to new ideas; besides, it'll be refreshing to get outsiders' takes on happenings in the Spalding family.

My theory involving the phone reading is an obvious choice to include as an example; I decide to add the television experience as well. I post my question on the message board the next morning at work:

"There's no such thing as coincidence, according to John Edward and Suzane. Everything happens for a reason!" I write. "The following happened to me ... Is there a reason?"

I check the message board daily. The numbers of responses I receive surprise me. The count goes both ways, pro and con.

Suzane Northrop's Message Board Posting

Renton tower, Tuesday, 18 February 2003

After everything that's happened over the years, I **listen** to the little voice in my head; it tells me I'm supposed to check out Suzane's website.

It's early morning; even though it appears a nice day is dawning, there's very little traffic this time of day. I turn towards the computer and type in the URL **www.theseance.com.**

The web site consists of approximately five areas of information. The one I'm pulled toward is the tab labeled **book tour and seminars.**

I notice a seminar date for the following Tuesday, February 25, 2003. It'll be held at the Four Seasons Olympic Hotel, downtown Seattle, at 7:00 p.m. till 9:30 p.m.

Wanda will be out of town that day, so I ask Rayshal if she'd like to attend a father and daughter dinner and **Spooks in Seattle seminar** the following week.

$$2/18/03 = 2+1+8+3 = \textbf{14}$$

I prepare for this seminar as I did for the seminar in 2002. I review my list of friends and loved ones who have passed. I look at their picture or other memory items, and give each one a few minutes of my time each day in loving thought and meditation.

There's only one thing I do different this time. I ask Sean to come through for his sister Rayshal! I feel it's the right thing to do.

The two of them were very close growing up together; besides, I'd received my validation from him the previous year over the phone.

Four Season Olympic Hotel, Tuesday night, February 25, 2003

We arrive at the hotel in plenty of time for a nice leisurely dinner, drinks and conversation; nevertheless, we're both contemplating what's going to happen over the next few hours.

The conference room has enough seating for approximately one hundred people. We take seats toward the back, on the far side of the room. "This is good," I whisper. "Less people mean a better chance of receiving a reading."

It begins almost the same as the previous seminar. I choose not to ask my question about the fireman. I sit back and enjoy the question & answer portion of the program.

During the final reading, I have a strong sensation the dead person (**DP**) she's making a connection with can be my brother Jack, who passed the previous year.

I count four possible validations called out to the audience. I get a slight nudge from Rayshal to raise my hand. I hesitate; I hold back because I want to hear one more validation to make sure.

Needless to say, several other people in the audience feel the validation is for them and raise their hand. I back down; I concede without even entering the process.

A **rule of thumb** at a seminar I forget to follow is this: If you feel in any possible way the message can be for you, **raise your hand!** This will alert the medium. They'll have to do their job, drawing out more information from the contact to see exactly who the message is for by offering more **personal validations.**

My own personal take on the process upstairs is this: The **DP's,** as Suzane lovingly refers to them, are waiting in line in various *related* groups with information to give out for validation purposes.

Sometimes these lines aren't as orderly as one might expect. The communication frequency vibrations from DP's are received by the medium in a similar way to multiple radio stations transmitting at the same time.

Try to imagine sitting in the middle of a busy Starbuck's in downtown Seattle. Close your eyes and listen to the amount of noise and energy throughout the room, and try to focus on the **strongest** voice or energy coming through.

It takes quite a bit of concentration and exerted energy to be successful. A medium, on the other hand, has to maintain this concentration level for longer periods of time, as well as providing a particular audience member with the information being told to them by a spirit from the other side.

Because of similarities in information, if you don't raise your hand to get into the game at the start, you prevent **your DP** from getting into the game on the other side.

On our way to Olympia one weekend, I mention to Wanda about my job in the next life. It's Sunday, May 26th, 2002. The time is 11:24 a.m. Wanda documents my thought on paper as I speak.

*"...with all of the confusion upstairs, pushing, shoving and wanting to be heard, along with my expertise in the field of Air Traffic control, I think I'll put in an early request to be a **Spirit Usher!**"*

$$11:24 = 1+2 = 3 \quad 1\ \&\ 4 = 14$$
$$5/26/2002 = 5+2+6 = 13 = 1+3 = 4 \quad 2+2 = 4 \quad (2)\ 4\text{'s} = 24$$

I truly believe my brother *Jack* is unable to make his connection because of my hesitation for one more piece of information. On the other hand, I prevent myself from receiving valuable information and validations I could've used to help his children cope with the loss of their father.

Despite the events noted above, the seminar went well. Neither of us received a reading; nevertheless, I believe Rayshal comes away with more understanding of the afterlife and how the process works.

I told her at dinner this seminar is meant to prepare her mind and heart to be open to belief. I want her to be the conduit, along with her brother, that Wanda and I will use after our time on Earth is over.

We're both happy for those who received messages from their loved ones. Just to be part of the experience, seeing and feeling the tears of joy and happiness, is enough to let you know that if you're willing to open your mind and heart to the experience, you too can have this sense of calm and comfort in knowing your loved ones are **still around you after death.**

After standing in line for a few minutes to have Suzane autograph our new books, we head to our car for the short drive home. The number **fourteen** rests quietly in my thought process as we steer the car onto the entry ramp to southbound Interstate 5.

February 25, 2003 = 2/25/2003 = 2+2+5+2+3 = **14**

Chapter Six

The Discovery

Renton tower, Wednesday morning, February 26, 2003
Once again, there're no airplanes flying this morning. The miserable February weather has been taking its toll.

"This'll be a good time to see what Suzane's latest book has to offer," I think aloud.

Everything is making sense as I continue reading each page. I've picked up similar information from other authors of previous books I've read.

Turning to page eighteen of the book, I see the narrative is about a belief in numbers as a valuable connection tool. "No kidding?" I joke. "I can think of a lot in my life!"

I focus on the next page, page **nineteen.** "What?" Oh, my gosh!" I exclaim. "It's my number theory I posted on the board!"

I didn't have to read the entire article to know what it was about; I automatically turn the page. The next story is about Sean's visit using our television set to let us know of his presence.

My heart begins to race; a shock moves through me like a bolt of lightning. If I'd been standing my legs would've buckled. I'm becoming familiar to this reaction when I receive forthright messages from Sean.

Tears fill my eyes and slowly run down my cheeks as all the joy and emotion I feel inside bubbles inside of me. I pick up the phone to call Wanda before she leaves for work, my hands trembling as I listen to the phone ring.

"Yeah, what do you want?" she answers sarcastically, knowing in advance I'm on the other end of the phone.

My mouth moves, but no sound comes out. I can't speak as I try to hold back the tears and emotion. All Wanda hears is muffled noises, and she instantly snaps alert. "What's wrong?" she asks nervously. Fraught with worry, she envisions her husband having a heart attack over the phone.

Finally, I regain the use of my vocal cords. "The book," I croak! "The book!"

Wanda is still unsure what's happening. "What book?" she asks.

"Suzane's book," I blurt out! I'm still in disbelief. "From last night!"

"What about it?" she questions; her response is quick. The tone in her voice indicates immediate interest in my news.

"We're in it!" I cry out. "Sean! The phone reading! My numbers theory! It's all here in the book; even the story about our television experience!"

"What?" she screams. "You're kidding?"

"Pages **nineteen** and **twenty**…it's all here!" I add.

Pages nineteen/twenty = 19/20 = 19+20 = **39**

39 =

3 March = the month Sean died

9 September = the month Sean is born

93 (reversed) = Year of Sean's death.

39 = Sean's name alphabet number placement

Luckily, I don't have any airplanes to deal with. Hanging up the phone, I sit in silence, attempting to absorb the meaning of the past few minutes.

I wanted Sean to come through in the worst way last night for his sister; in addition, I was hoping he could add a few more pieces to the puzzle in regards to his passing.

Needless to say, I'll accept this grandiose entrance – **in black and white** – as another validation from him, and I'll do what I feel is necessary by the thought messages going through my mind:

Sean's time on Earth is memorialized on his gravestone. Now, thanks to Suzane Northrop, his time on Earth is also memorialized in print. He'll be remembered long after my passing, as well as by others not yet born.

Suzane had felt the connection between Sean and I so moving and so important, she used two pages of valuable space in her two hundred and sixty seven page book.

Unfortunately, I didn't know about these pages the previous night. While I held the book awaiting her autograph, I could've hugged her right there and said **thank-you!**

The time is right to call Sean's mother

My heart feels I'd be doing the right thing. Pat and I haven't spoken to each other for almost ten years. I need to bring her up-to-date on everything that's happening with Sean at present, as well as the past few years.

This information belongs to her as well as me. Besides, it helped to move me forward in my life; it can surely help her move forward in her life. It'll also help assuage any remaining issues involving the loss of our child.

I sense I'm **destined** to make the call; I feel it's been prearranged in advance.

There're too many distractions calling from work, so I postpone it until I get home.

The clock shows 8:15 a.m. Wanda is already on her way to work. I'm still hyped! I need to talk with someone with an interest in this who will listen.

49

"Greg, am I catching you at a bad time?" I ask my brother. My eyes scan the skies outside the tower window. I glance at the D-Brite radar screen and check for aircraft.

"When my brother calls me on my cell phone at work, something must've happened," he replies. "Tell me it isn't bad news?"

"I called to let you know you're famous!" Going right for his jugular, I explain, "You're mentioned in a book!"

"What are you talking about?" he asks anxiously. If anything makes Greg sound important, he's interested. I proceed to fill in the blanks. I refresh his memory of the night we sat in the bedroom to listen to Sean's phone reading.

"Try to remember your theory on the missing number **fourteen?**" I say.

For the moment, he's gone way past thinking about numbers and an abstract theory.

"My name is really in her book?" he asks again. His thoughts are about a new career unfolding before him; his mind drifts ahead to a place with $ signs!

I burst his bubble before it gets out of hand. "Not your name," I correct. "It's a reference to it. She used the word **brother** to be noncommittal," I explain.

The call is over within minutes. After performing a few of the duties in the tower I'm being paid to perform, my cell phone rings. I look on the caller ID screen and see Greg's name.

"Tell me you didn't quit your day job already?" I quip.

Because his theory on the number fourteen had been so successful, he decided to do a little more calculating.

"Do you have a pencil and paper?" he asks.

"Yeah, why?" I ask hesitantly. I'm still not sure where he's going.

He begins to provide a few more tidbits on why he believes he's part of this unfolding psychic mystery; namely, his birth date, along with the alphabet number placement for the words **brother and Sean.**

I didn't want to tell him I'd already computed the numbers for Sean's name, so I just kept quiet and continued to write as directed.

Greg feels the added information can be important to my research. His assumption is correct; it adds more pieces to the puzzle and brings it closer to completion.

Greg was born:
9/5/52 = 9/5 = 9+5 = **14**
9/5/52 = 9+5+5+2 = 21 = 2+1 = **3**
3 = March
Sean died 3/**14**/93

Alphabet placement:
SEAN = 19+5+1+14 = **39**
BROTHER = 2+18+15+20+8+5+18 = 86 = 8+6 = **14**
39/14 = 3/14/93

Book Placement:
Pages 19 & 20 = 19+20= **39**

Des Moines, Washington, later that afternoon
The phone rings three times before a female voice answers. I know it isn't Pat, so I leave my name and number and ask the lady to tell Pat I'm calling about Sean. I want her to be a little prepared on the reason for my call if and when she returns it.

"Please tell her I have some information I need to share with her," I add.

My phone rings ten minutes later. I recognize Pat's Caribbean accent.

"Pat," I said, "thanks for returning my call."

"No problem," she responds. "What's going on?" Her voice sounds casual, as though we speak on a regular basis.

I delay the inevitable by making small talk. Finally, I ask her to get a sheet of paper and pencil; I also suggest she might want to sit down.

"Are you familiar with the *'Crossing Over with John Edward,'* show on television?" I ask, my voice a little hesitant.

"Yes!" comes her avid response. "I haven't seen it yet, but I've wanted to watch it for some time now. That kind of stuff **really interests me.**"

"Good," I reply. The tension I felt while making the phone call slowly subsides.

I start to think the conversation is going to be easier than expected. I presume Sean has been working overtime to make this contact as painless as possible.

"Growing up in Trinidad made me quite aware of things like that," she went on to say. "Don't tell me you've forgotten about the locals and their belief in Voodoo and Black Magic?"

"Oh, no, I still remember it was going on when I was there." I respond.

The best way to begin a story is at the beginning, so I mention *Suzane Northrop.* Pat lets me know right away she's familiar with her work also.

We talk for almost forty-five minutes. I give her the name of Suzane's book so she can purchase a copy for herself. I also play the tape of my phone reading from the radio station the previous year.

"I'll send you a copy, along with notes from our discussion on my number theory," I said.

"That'll be nice," she agrees.

I'm still curious about Suzane's reference to a fishing pole, and her interpretation: *how Sean and I enjoyed doing this together.*

After hearing it again as I played it for Pat, I begin to think there might be another answer.

"This is the only part on the tape that doesn't make any sense to us," I confess. "The only possible explanation we can figure is the skiing trip I took him on where he broke his leg."

Sean vowed never to go skiing again after the accident. I feel Suzane may have **misinterpreted** the ski poles as they were being shown to her.

Pat's response catches me off guard. "Sean use to go fishing with Rob quite a lot," she states. "As a matter of fact, the three of us ice fished together."

The wheels in my brain begin to turn. "If the fishing pole reference is for your side of the family, maybe the part about having a brother, totally opposite in character, is also a validation for **your son Josh** – as well as Travis?"

Sean grew up with two fathers. I'm his biological Dad, while Rob, Pat's second husband, is his stepfather. Because both families accepted this fact, even Sean, he'd been able to grow up in a comfortable home environment and live a nice life knowing he has two fathers, without the usual backstabbing that takes place in divorced households.

Suzane wouldn't be aware of Sean's past family history, or the unique relationship between the families. She'd only know the energy is trying to communicate with his **father!**

Before hanging up with Pat, I let her know I believe Sean prearranged our conversation. "This phone call had been set up some time ago," I said.

She let me know the flowers I send twice a year are nice. She also mentions how Sean loved butterflies and the color blue.

"I've noticed several times, when I visit his grave, an all blue butterfly buzzes around me," she describes. "I know its Sean having fun at my expense; he's letting me know things are okay where he's at."

I find myself looking for this blue butterfly every time I'm outdoors in the Pacific Northwest. I know someday he's going to make his appearance and say hello.

Knowing Sean the way I do, and the way his mind works, he'll probably be surrounded by thirteen other butterflies of various colors.

One blue butterfly
One = **1**   blue = 40 = 4+0 = **4**   butterfly = 129= 1+2 = **3**   9 = **9**
3/**14**/93

Chapter Seven
Thanks, But What Does It Mean?

Des Moines, Thursday morning 2:00 a.m., February 27, 2003,
My eyes open; I can't sleep. Something is still eating away at me. The book revelation is fantastic; nevertheless, it isn't the end of the journey – I'm sure of that. This puzzle still has a few more **missing pieces.**

I put on my slippers and pad to the living room. I sit down in the dark room in a chair facing the picture window. The storage cabinet in my mind starts to open; the clues from past years begin to cascade through my brain like a waterfall.

"What am I forgetting?" I think aloud.

I see a large number **14** in my thought imagery. It stands out foremost among all the other clues. I scribble numbers on a blank sheet of paper; I write down the dates of the seminars I've attended.

"Why's Portland, Oregon coming to mind?" I mumble.

The light switch in my brain clicks on; I remember Suzane has one more seminar to complete before her five-hour extravaganza in Las Vegas with John Edward and two other world-class mediums.

This last seminar will be held at the Radisson Hotel, in downtown Portland, on Friday, February 28th. I place this date along with the other mix of numbers on paper. I move the clues around as best I can. I'm still missing something…but what?

All of a sudden, a burst of bright energy fills my mind. The numbers on the paper seem to leap off the page and swirl in this mass of energy! Everything makes perfect sense – almost everything, that is.

"Sean is sending me on a mission," I say aloud as I slowly nod my head affirmatively.

I play out the following as I envision it in my mind: I'll attend the Portland seminar on Friday night; I'll leave right after work on Friday morning. At the seminar I can thank Suzane for including my articles in her book.

I'll also pick up a few extra autographed copies of her book following the seminar. I'll send one to Pat and a thank-you copy to Greg for his help in trying to solve this mystery.

The final outcome, unfortunately, is still uncertain. "I'll have to leave that ending up to **Sean**," I murmur, as if I'm in conversation with my own thought patterns.

Wanda walks out of the bedroom rubbing her eyes. She looks down the hallway and sees me in the chair writing.

"What's going on?" she asks, her eyes glancing quickly to the wall clock.

"I can't sleep," I answer. "I keep getting this feeling I'm suppose to do something."

"Do something like what?" she asks.

"I think I'm supposed to go to Suzane's seminar in Portland this Friday." My voice is hinting for an approval.

Wanda has always supported the readings and my adventures into psychic belief.

"If you think you should go, then go," she encourages. She also recommends spending the night so I won't be too tired to drive home after the seminar.

"Good idea! I'll make a reservation at the same hotel, and I'll order my seminar ticket later this morning."

Since Portland is a five-hour roundtrip, it made perfect sense to spend the night and drive home the next morning. Besides, I don't know what's going to happen at the seminar; it might be best if I stay off of the road until the next day.

I pose one more question to Wanda before she retires back to the bedroom.

"Do you know what this Friday is?" I ask. "No, what?" she asks with a slight yawn.

"Two weeks before the tenth anniversary of his death," I state. "Two weeks is fourteen – and there's the number **fourteen** again!"

"Then by all means, **you should go!**"

Wanda turns towards the bedroom. "According to my calculations," I begin, "Friday marks two hundred and forty nine days since Suzane's first seminar; the one we attended in Seattle."

Wanda stops abruptly, before turning and looking back blankly in my direction. It's too early in the morning to toss out formulas and numbers. "Meaning?" she asks.

"These numbers represent the month and day Sean was born," I answer. "Maybe this means a rebirth of some type…or a new beginning for all of us?"

At this time of day, the only thing Wanda knows for certain is 5 a.m. is right around the corner. Wordlessly, she closes the bedroom door behind her.

I know Sean wants me in Portland on Friday sitting in the seminar audience. What will happen is anyone's guess; at this point, I only know one thing – **I have to be there!**

First Seminar– 6/24/02
Second Seminar– 2/25/03
Third Seminar– 2/28/03
246 Days between First and Second Seminar
246 = **6/24** – Date of First Seminar
2+4+6 = 12 = 1+2 = **3** Month Sean **Died**
24 = Day of Sean's **Birth**
249 Days between First and Third Seminar
249 = **9/24** Sean's **Birth Month** and **Day**

Radisson Hotel, Portland, Oregon, February 28th, 2003

I arrive at the hotel Friday around 12:30 p.m. Walking up to the front desk to check-in and get my room key, I glance over my right shoulder and notice the hotel's large information board across from me.

In bold letters at the top: **Suzane Northrop seminar 7:00 – 9:30 p.m.**

I make a mental note of the name of the conference room for later use. "Your key, sir," says the desk clerk, interrupting my train of thought. "Your room number is on the card and the elevator is right behind you."

"Thank you," I acknowledge, reaching for my bag and turning in the direction of the elevator. As I'm walking onto the unoccupied elevator, I reach to push the floor button when I realize I forgot what room the clerk assigned me. Pulling the key out of my shirt pocket, I read aloud, "Room 325!"

I push button number **3,** and the elevator begins its slow ascent.

"Third floor...hmm...number three – for **March!**"

When the elevator door opens on the third floor, I follow the signs leading to my room. Walking around the corner, I notice the door for Rooms **324** and **325** are side by side.

Another thought makes its way into my mind: "Number twenty five...hmm...**twenty four** must've been occupied already," I think aloud. Otherwise, Sean would've made sure the desk clerk knew in advance I wanted this particular room.

Things are shaping up quite well. Everything appears to be set up **in advance.** I wonder what else Sean has arranged?

After dropping off my bags in the room, I go downstairs for a bite in the hotel's main dining room. Quiet and deserted for a Friday afternoon, I wait momentarily at the front to be seated. Once seated, I note that I have the whole restaurant to myself, except for an elderly couple seated in the far corner.

"They're probably the couple in room 324," I think to myself.

After giving the waiter my order, my thoughts fast-forward six hours. I know my own reasons for being here; nevertheless, the feelings I've become accustom to over the years **tell a different story.**

"Here you go, sir," says the waiter. "Hope you enjoy your meal." As I begin to eat, I allow my thoughts to blur out any activity taking place around me.

Before heading back to my room, I walk down to the conference room where the seminar will take place. I notice it's quite small by comparison to the conference room at the Seattle conference three days earlier.

The chairs are arranged in rows of eighteen, with a break in the middle, to allow access for Suzane to get up and down the aisle during the readings.

With only five rows of chairs in the room, I know it'll be a much smaller audience than the Tuesday night group in Seattle.

There's a better chance of a reading by Suzane when the body count is low, because fewer **DP's** on the other side show up as well.

A representative for the *Jodere Group*, a book publishing group sponsoring the event, sees me standing at the door entrance and asks if he can help me with anything.

"By chance, is Suzane's assistant Linda here?" I ask.

I was hoping she could arrange a little extra time with Suzane for me after the seminar, so I could share with her my feelings about my family's validations put forth in her book.

When I give him my name, he looks at me with a puzzled expression.

"Weren't you at the Seattle seminar the other day?" he asks.

"Yes," I reply.

"Linda is in Las Vegas," he advises. "She's helping everyone get ready for the big show tomorrow night. Can I help?"

I begin to explain my intentions for attending this seminar when he interrupts me partway through.

"Yes, now I know the name," he states. "I got an email this morning from my San Diego office saying you'd like a little free time with Suzane – something about her book?"

"That's right," I agree.

I had called Jodere Group in San Diego the morning I made reservations for the seminar. I explained my situation and asked if something could be arranged with Suzane.

"It's hard for us to get in touch with her when she's traveling," was the courteous 'I can't do it' response. "I would suggest sending an email to her assistant Linda with your request."

Fortunately, this guy didn't think my request would pose any problems; especially after I suggested I might linger around during the book signing after the seminar, angling to be the last one in line.

"I'm sure Suzane will be happy to do that," he responds. "I took a copy of the company email to her room. This way, she'll be aware of what's going on, and allow a few extra minutes afterwards."

I walk back to the room to rest before the seminar. Another thought about Sean doing more advance preparation work crosses my mind.

A card on top of the television set advertises the new *"Harry Potter movie"* on pay per view.

What the heck, I've read all of the latest books and I've seen the first movie; in fact, I'd be considered an avid *Harry Potter* fan. Besides, it's an entertaining way to kill a few hours.

Chapter Eight
End of the Rainbow: He's Listening

Radisson Hotel, Friday night 6:15 p.m., room 325

Before leaving the room I speak to Sean: "I'm here son, because of you! My goal is a short talk with Suzane, and to get a copy of her book for your mom. I don't know if you have plans for anything else to happen; whatever the case may be, I'm happy for the validation in the book and for the opportunity just to be here."

When the elevator door opens to the main lobby, I step out, turn to my right, and walk toward the conference room in the back of the hotel. There's no one around as I proceed down the long corridor. I express my thoughts out loud one final time as I near the conference room: "If you have any plans in store for me tonight, son, that's fine – it's your show," I said. "If not, thanks for being with me and getting me here."

During the next forty-five minutes, I sit quietly in the small conference room watching the guests arrive and take their seats; I wonder who'll be sitting around me once the seminar gets underway, and how close their personal experience will mirror my own.

I've learned from past seminars that the seating arrangement seems to be arranged by the ones above. They exercise their ability to put thought messages in your mind as you walk through the door.

People will group together by the way a loved one departed this world. For some reason, this makes it easier for Suzane to make her connections, as the DP's intermingle in her thought process.

The host is the man I spoke with earlier in the day, Ira. Striding to the front of the room, he reads the format for the night's event before introducing Suzane Northrop. Only forty-eight people are present; nevertheless, they enthusiastically make their acceptance and appreciation for Suzane's work known; she enters the room to loud, thunderous applause!

As she walks upon the stage glancing around the room, the applause dies down. "Wow, what a small audience," she remarks. "This is bad for me – but good for you folks!"

The actual reading of messages, or validations, takes place after the break. This is always the final part of her seminar, and usually lasts about one hour to one hour and fifteen minutes.

A ten minute meditation is conducted by her before the readings begin. This is done to relax our mind and bodies, thus making it easier for a spiritual visit, **or connection.**

As always, Suzane has no control over who stops by for a visit, or for that matter, who in the audience will actually receive a message. She can only assure there'll be visitors from the other side on this night.

About fifteen minutes into the readings, a sensation passes through my body. Suzane is at the front of the room, toward the corner, completing a message to a couple seated two rows ahead of me.

Once the connection is finished and the *spirit visitor's energy* has departed, Suzane prepares herself to receive the next *energy form*, along with the message it came to give.

Her back and forth pacing motion begins to increase; her mind is starting to receive new information from the other side. She stops abruptly!

"I'm hearing the name, Rayshal or Rachel?" she announces.

I nearly fall off my chair as my legs go limp; my hand rises in the air for quick identification. "Rayshal is my daughter!" I reply.

"Does she have a brother who's passed?" she asks.

By now, she's moved to the center of the room. She's standing next to the raised stage area awaiting my response; her head is tipped to one side, her right hand covers her brow as her eyes look in my direction.

"Yes," I confirm anxiously. I know the entity conversing with Suzane is Sean. He's using his sister's name so there's no mistake about it.

My mind can't help but reflect back to the seminar in Seattle. I asked Sean in a mental prayer if he'd come through for his sister. I guess there had to be a reason he chose not to come through at that time, even though she was in the audience.

Suzane begins her pacing once again in front of the stage area. "He's showing me boats – lots of boats," she explains. Her right arm circles over her head in an arch- like motion. "Do you live by boats?" she asks.

"Yes!" comes my avid response. "There's a large marina right down the street, about a quarter of a mile."

Because of this validation, I know Sean is aware of our moves around the country and our progressions through this life since his passing. The marina is one of the areas I use for my jogging routine. I jog along the pier where the boats are moored and the fishermen cast their lines.

While jogging, my mind will wander to whatever thought or emotion flows through at the time.

I picture Sean aboard my sister Bonnie's boat. This took place in the late eighties, after his high school graduation, and before he and his mom's family moved out of state to Alabama.

My family and I flew back to the states, from American Samoa in the South Pacific, to attend his high school graduation. At that time, my sister asked if he'd like to spend some time on her boat, after Wanda, the kids and I left Ohio to fly back to Pago Pago...

The image of Sean on my sister's boat fades quickly. I see Suzane once again at the front of the room. She's stopped pacing; her brain waves seem to be receiving more information from the other side.

My reading continues with more specifics on Sean's death. The questions flow in rapid fire succession.

"I'm sensing a very fast passing. He's here…Boom! He's there." She continues along this train of thought before I can validate the statement.

"There's a loud crash – very loud!" she says. "He's also telling me there's a lot of other noise involved." Her pacing stops as quickly as it starts; her eyes glance in my direction. "Can you validate any of this?" she asks.

"Yes," I agree. I begin shaking like a leaf on an autumn day. The hairs stand on my body. I envision the crash in my mind; I've seen this vision many times before over the last ten years.

There's a slight pause in her delivery; I quickly jot down a few specific notes on my writing pad. I don't want to take any of my focus away when she's talking. I need to hear the exact words being conveyed.

"I'm sensing a similarity in character," she continues. "Was he a lot like you? I'm sensing the word…stubborn!"

I smile. "I'd say yes, at least on my part."

Once again, Suzane starts circling around the front of the room; her arms move to the rhythm of her thought patterns. "He's showing me a boy much younger than he," she relays. "Is he your only son… or does he have a brother?"

I recall a similar question being asked during my phone reading with her in Seattle the previous year. "He has a brother," I reply. "But he's from a different marriage."

"Is this brother still alive?" she asks. Her forehead wrinkles; her face reflects the intense concentration taking place within her mind as she tries to sort out the puzzle.

"Yes," I offer.

"But he's much, much younger than this son?" she continues, hoping a validation from me confirms what Sean is showing her.

"Yes," I agree, with a little extra emotion. "He's eleven years younger."

The audience members contently watch and listen to the reading at hand. As far as Suzane is concerned, she isn't the least bit surprised my validations from Sean are continuing. She's seen this before at other seminars, where one family will monopolize the stage, while other families sit quietly in the gallery and patiently await their own messages from a loved one.

"I'm sensing your son is deeply affected by the loss of his brother," she conveys. "He's showing me something like wandering! It's like his brother still isn't sure of the direction in life he should be following."

Her pacing stops abruptly once again; she awaits my validation to the message before continuing.

"Yes, yes!" I confirm wholeheartedly, my head nodding in agreement.

My thoughts flash back to Travis. He's a graduate of the Seattle Art Institute. It's been three years since his graduation, and he's still unable to decide on a career path. I keep forgetting he's only twenty-three. The training he received will last a life time. Unfortunately, I continue to remind him monthly about his talents and abilities as I write out a check for my portion of his student loan repayment.

My mind recalls Suzane's mention of a fishing pole the previous year. I remember how that message could apply to Sean's mother's side of the family as well.

I think of Pat's son Josh, and wonder if his situation is also similar to Travis. Sean knows I'll pass along any information I receive to his mother. He's possibly using the word "brother" in this instance, so the validation can apply to both boys.

65

"He's showing me the ocean or the seas!" she expresses. "Like someone is out at sea for a long time...or even lost at sea?" Her voice hesitates; she's unclear at this point what she's being shown.

I'd forgotten about being on a seven-month Mediterranean Sea cruise during my Marine Corps stint. It took place almost a year before Sean's birth in nineteen sixty-seven.

"My son's girlfriend has a father who works aboard a ship," I offer. "He's gone quite often out to sea!"

Suzane responds quickly. "I'll take that as a validation."

The next question catches me by surprise. It's the second time she's been able to come up with an actual name of a family member; in addition, she's able to reveal his relationship to me.

"Do you have a brother, Greg or Craig?" she asks. Her pacing begins a little slower around the front of the room.

"Yes!" I blurt quickly. "My brother's name is Greg! This is the same brother you reference in your book." In fact, both names she referenced are correct. My biological brother is Greg; my sister's husband is Craig.

I think back to the animosity I still hold against Craig. Craig had dissuaded Bonnie from attending Sean's funeral, despite the pleas from our sister Diane, along with many of her office coworkers. They all tried to let her know she'd be making a big mistake and live to regret it.

Her husband felt it wasn't worth the $250 airfare in flying from Ohio to Alabama to attend the funeral, even though they could well afford it with their combined six-figure income.

If I'd acknowledged his name, Sean possibly would've conveyed a message to move on with my life and let go of this anger. But how can I forget when someone tells you your son isn't worth an airline ticket?

My sister is aware of my feelings. She totally regrets the day she listened to her husband and made that choice in her life.

My remark about Suzane citing my brother Greg in her book surprises her.

"If I referenced him in my book; then I guess I should know the answer to the question already," she chuckles. The audience laughs at her comment. "Are you aware your son has visited you before?" she asks as she stops at the front of the aisle close to where I'm sitting. She stares in my direction awaiting a response.

I reflect back to the incident in front of the television set. I completely forget about the dream I had several years earlier, or the feelings I get when I sense his presence around me offering clues and information on a continual basis.

"Yes!" I said.

"He's telling me he knew he's going to have a short life on this Earth," she relays. "Were you aware of this?"

Her eyes focus in my direction; her on-again, off-again movements have stopped. I can feel the eyes of the audience members staring in my direction as well.

The content of her message throws me for a loop. Once again, I'm caught with my defenses down. I completely forget about Sean's three previous accidents during his younger years.

"No," I reply. A knot forms in the pit of my stomach; I jot down a quick note to the reference.

After delivering this message, Suzane takes a brief pause as her brain cells reload with new information.

"He's showing me medals…lots of medals, she states. "Did you, or anyone in your family, earn or possess a lot of medals?"

I was in the Marine Corps from 1964-1968. I was stationed at the Naval Air Station in Trinidad during the Vietnam War, and my tour of duty there lasted approximately two years before I was transferred stateside to Camp Lejeunne, North Carolina. It was there I met and dated Sean's mother Patricia.

The military frowned on any soldier marrying at a duty station outside the United States, whatever the reason. If you tried to fight it or threatened any action such as writing a congressman, they'd quickly end your tour of duty and ship you back stateside.

Fortunately, Pat worked for an airline company in Trinidad. A flight back to the United States for her and her mother didn't cost a large amount. Much to the disappointment of the commanding officer and his staff, we postponed the marriage until my tour of duty ended in Trinidad.

I married Sean's mother before reporting for duty in North Carolina. Nevertheless, the military was able to separate us a year later for seven months when I deployed on a Mediterranean cruise with the Sixth Fleet.

"I received two or three medals from my military service," I answer Suzane. "But that's not a lot!"

Suzane abruptly stops her pacing around the front of the conference room after I reply. Her right hand again rests above her brow, but she suddenly gestures with the same hand, moving it up and down on the left front side of her chest – where medals would be worn.

"He's showing me a man in uniform with a chest full of medals," she reiterates.

"The only person who comes to mind is a military friend I knew when I was stationed in Trinidad," I offer. "He died in Vietnam, but I've thought about him a lot over the years," I add.

Private Mitchel... He was a young, robust black male, who reminded me of a black Curly from the Three Stooges. He and I became very good friends during our time spent together on the island.

We arrived in Trinidad about the same time, assigned to the same platoon, thus allowing our liberty calls into the capital city of Port-of-Spain to be an adventure together. The two other Marines we hung out with gave him the nickname Pea Brain! This name stuck with him for his entire time spent in Trinidad. In fact, he chose to use it as his personal introduction to the ladies at the local bars during liberty calls.

"Well, he must've earned a lot of medals over there," Suzane replies. "His whole chest is covered with them now. He says 'hello.'" Her head nods in my direction as the message is delivered.

I smile and nod my head in return. I thank Pea Brain for taking the time to stop by and say hello.

"Why am I seeing the state of Michigan?" she asks, stopping near the podium. She glances back in my direction. "Am I still with you?" she inquires.

"My dad had a war buddy who lived in Michigan. We went to visit them a lot when I was a kid," I reply.

I'd forgotten about Rayshal's trip to Michigan several months earlier. She went on a business trip while driving back to Ohio to visit my sister Diane and her husband Bob. I wonder if any more validations concerning his sister would've come from Sean, and if the reading would have gone in a different direction, had I used Rayshal's trip as my validation.

"Are the husband and wife both passed?" Suzane asks.

"Yes, I believe so," I acknowledge.

"They both say 'hello,'" she relays.

After this last validation, Suzane moves to the other side of the room; the thought process in her mind senses a change in energy. My reading is over, while a new energy source tries to connect with his or her loved one in the audience.

I sit quietly for a moment trying to absorb what has just taken place. A heavy load has been lifted from my mind. I think about the meaning of it all, and how it will affect Wanda and the rest of the family when I return home.

Silently, I offer a prayer and thank Sean for coming through. I thank him for using his sister's name to begin the process and get the ball rolling.

I wish this had taken place in Seattle, when Rayshal was in the audience. Unfortunately, our time is not their time; we get the message when they feel we're prepared to receive and handle it.

Suzane is now standing at the front of the room. She's on the far side of the aisle and making another connection to a family in search of their own lost loved one.

As I'm listening to the message, she suddenly interrupts the validation process. "Excuse me," she apologizes. "I'll be right back."

She strides purposefully across the front of the room and down the aisle in my direction. She stops next to my chair. I look up at her; my eyes intently search Suzane's for an explanation.

"Your son asked me to come over and give you a big hug," she explains while reaching down, wrapping her arms around me and squeezing me tight in a big hug.

I hug her back. "Thanks," I reply. "I really needed that!" My thoughts hug Sean in return.

Two weeks before the tenth anniversary of his death
Two weeks = fourteen days

14

Chapter Nine

New Discovery

Radisson Hotel, Portland, Friday night, 9:55 p.m.

After the seminar, I remain seated in my chair and wait for the book signing line to dwindle. Glancing down at my notes, my thoughts recall each validation I scribbled on the paper; I feel their impact once again on my life.

Glimpsing over my shoulder, I see the line has trickled down to just four people. I stand up and walk to the back of the short line.

Suzane smiles at a lady as she hands back her book, thanking her for attending the seminar. At long last, I'm here. It's just Suzane at the table, me, and Ira the Jodere representative standing in the doorway.

I set my stack of pre-purchased books on the table for her autograph. Looking up, she smiles as I introduce myself.

"Is it okay if I sit down and show you some of the clues that led me to this seminar?"

"Sure," she agrees with interest. "You did get a long reading tonight, didn't you?" she states rhetorically.

"I sure did!" I respond. Pulling up a chair alongside her, I place my tablet on the table with the list of clues I had organized before coming downstairs.

"First, I'd like to thank you for including a part of my story in your book," I begin.

"That's quite alright," she replies.

"Second, did you put my story on pages **19** and **20** for a reason?" I ask.

"No!" she replies quickly. "It wasn't intentional at all. Why?"

I explain how the numbers add up to the month and year of Sean's death. I also point out his name totals **39** in their alphabet letter placement. Her eyes gaze down at the numbers on the tablet; a smile creeps across her face.

We continue to go down my list of clues together. I bring her attention to the date of each of her seminars, pointing out how the date totals fourteen in my number theory.

"Tonight is two weeks before the tenth anniversary of his death," I explain. "Two weeks is actually fourteen days."

Suzane pulls the tablet closer to her, her eyes scanning quickly up and down the page. She looks in awe and amazement at the clues; her head shakes slowly back and forth as she begins comprehending what she's reading.

Most people will conclude that everything just happened that way, but of course, I know from her book **everything happens for a reason.**

I'm hopeful Suzane leaves Portland with a burgeoning belief in her own book theory, and that she'll take a small part of Sean and I home with her to New York.

The Jodere representative Ira walks toward the table. I choose not to overstay my welcome. I know Suzane's energy level is almost drained after each seminar; it takes a lot out of her to communicate with the other side.

I offer to send a copy of my *list of clues* to her assistant Linda so she can study this list closer once she's refreshed. "That'll be great," she agrees. "She'll see that I get it."

I stand up to leave and shake her hand good-bye. Upon grasping her hand I immediately sense a connection between Sean, Suzane and myself; a bond of energy that will never be broken. I can't help but feel we'll be seeing a lot more of each other in the near future.

Back at my room, I'm still riding on a cloud. I call Wanda and try to read the scribbling on my note pad the best I can.

"She actually said Rayshal's name?" Wanda asks.

"Yes," I reply. "She also mentioned Greg and Craig."

I bring up how I wish she'd been here to experience it with me. Nevertheless, we'll both enjoy the moment together for what it is, and allow Sean his own reasons for coming through at this time.

After hanging up the phone, I decide to go downstairs to the lounge for a quiet drink before retiring. It's a little crowded when I walk in, but I find a seat at the bar next to a young couple I noticed at the seminar.

Within a few minutes, the girl turns to me and asks, "Aren't you the one who had a long reading from your son?" she asks.

"Yes, that's me," I reply.

I decide to open up a little more and give them some inside information to the reason I'm at the seminar on this particular night. After sharing a short version of my story, I let them know the importance of the number fourteen, and why I feel I had a reading on this night.

Her name is Courtney, and her husband's name is Ryan. He shares a story about a dinner they missed with Suzane at his mother's house back on the East coast.

"My mom is a good friend of Suzane," he said. "In addition, my step dad owns a radio station where she's been a guest several times. The on-air readings are very popular with his listening audience."

As his story goes, the two of them flew back east to visit his mom. Their first night was to involve dinner with his parents, with Suzane as a special guest. Unfortunately, Ryan and Courtney encountered unforeseen travel problems, causing a very lengthy delay arriving at both the airport, as well as on their trip from the airport to his mother's house. As it turned out, they arrived at the house two hours late, and like Elvis, Suzane had already left the building, much to their disappointment.

Ryan then shares a bit of information that aptly demonstrates why our paths are destined to cross on this night, and why our two stories converge. They came to the seminar with hopes of contacting Ryan's sister. She was living in Florida at the time of her accident, and like Sean, she also died in an auto mishap. Today marks the **fourteenth year** anniversary of her death.

Speechless, the three of us just stare at one another after Ryan mentions the number fourteen. Courtney and I both reach for paper and pencil to exchange phone numbers and e-mail addresses. Having just left the seminar, we all know **everything happens for a reason!**

Before leaving the hotel the next morning, I remember to call Sean's mom. I want her to know he came through with messages that will surely have an impact on her family as well.

Sean's step dad Rob answers the phone. I briefly mention the seminar, asking if Pat had said anything to him regarding our phone conversation three days earlier.

"No?" he responds, his voice sounding like a question. It also has a slightly harsh, negative tone.

Hesitating, I sense I might have said something or relayed information that I shouldn't have.

"Okay, then...can I, uh, speak to Pat, please?" I ask.

A split second later she's on the phone. Her demeanor isn't as upbeat as I remember three days earlier. While she listens to what I have to say, her carefree, receptive attitude from the other day is gone. I feel like a stranger that's been away for almost ten years.

"Oh well," I sigh, hanging up the phone. "I passed on the message like the book says, and as Sean wanted."

I met Wanda, her mother, Rayshal and John a few hours later, at Shari's restaurant in Olympia, to share my experience firsthand. I'd already expected John's skepticism on the events.

A few days later, I mail a package to Pat. It contains a copy of my phone reading with Suzane, a personally autographed book, and a handwritten transcript from the reading I received at the seminar in Portland, Oregon.

Renton tower, 2 months later, Wednesday, April 30, 2003

During a lull in flight traffic, a thought goes through my mind to check Suzane's web site. Once logged on, I go right to the message board where the various subject material is highlighted. Scanning the topics a little longer than usual, one entitled *"John Holland,"* catches my attention. I'm unfamiliar with this name, so I read a few of the messages relating to John Holland.

He's another top-notch medium like Suzane and John Edward, and he also participated in the Las Vegas extravaganza. I note that he'll be in Seattle on Saturday, May 03, 2003, or in three days. I order my tickets just seconds after leaving the web site.

John Holland seminar, Saturday, May 03, 2003

The seminar begins at 10:00 a.m., and it's scheduled to last almost two and a half hours. John begins by talking about his life as a medium, and how he refused to embrace this gift for much of his young adult life. However, a near fatal car accident was to become the catalyst to change all that.

He shares a story about how one day while killing some time spent shopping "a feeling comes over me to buy a certain item I'm looking at. I don't know why – I just know I have to!"

Continuing, he explains how this item he purchased is carried from show to show until its meaning is revealed to him. He usually gives it to an audience member during his seminar.

Before the actual readings get underway John takes an intermission, where he signs copies of his new book: *"born KNOWING."*

Wanda and I are at the end of the line. As we approach the table, I hand him the book I purchased earlier to sign. I thank him for coming to Seattle, adding that I found the presentation about his life intriguing.

"Thank you, I appreciate that," he replies.

Before he can sign my book, I tell him the last medium I'd seen was *Suzane Northrop*, and add how she mentions a few of my experiences in her latest book on pages **19** and **20.** "If you're interested in reading it," I offer.

Wanda and I are astounded by his response. He drops his book signing pen, and jerks backward in his chair; his eyes focus intently on Wanda and I, then points a finger in my direction.

"You're him!" he says in a loud voice.

"Him?" I say, startled.

"Isn't the article in her book about your son and a TV?" he asks questioningly.

"Yes, that's me," I reply. The thought of another well-known medium hearing about my son and I sends a wave of goose bumps over my entire body.

"Suzane uses your story quite a lot back east in her seminar discussions," he adds.

"Oh, really?" I muse.

"I'll be talking with her on Monday," he informs. "I'll tell her you said hello."

"Thanks, that'll be nice." I agree. I shake his hand after he hands me the autographed book.

A passing thought of another validation from Sean traverses my mind. I begin to think maybe Suzane actually studied my list of clues I sent to her assistant.

If she's using this story about Sean and me, we must have captured her attention. I also hope she'll be an integral part of getting our story told one day in print.

During the readings, John comes close to our section of the audience with a validation. "I'm either in this row with the '**numbers man**,'" he calls out, "or I'm in the row behind him."

A Canadian father and his daughter had driven to Seattle to attend the seminar in hopes of contacting her mother. Their trip isn't in vain. The mother comes through with validations for her husband as well as her daughter.

In addition, the mother reveals a validation about a red heart-shaped locket important in her daughter's life. This makes John pause in his delivery for just a moment.

Walking over to a small table with a little gift box on it, he opens it to show the audience a red heart-shaped locket.

"I guess your mother wanted me to give you this," he says, stepping off the stage and handing the girl the locket.

_____

Later that day I work a closing shift at the tower, and after work I'm still thinking about the Holland seminar. It's 9:15 p.m., and I'm remembering a lady at the seminar who sat next to us that had lost three children in one auto accident. At the seminar Wanda and I both focused thinking positive thoughts to help get a message from the other side about her children.

I even ask Sean if he can help get someone through for her. Sadly, nobody comes through. She leaves the seminar as depressed as when she arrived.

Driving home now, I thank Sean for trying to bring the children through. I concluded, along with a later agreement from Wanda, the lady didn't receive her validation because she isn't ready to receive it. She needs to work through her loss and grieving process a little more.

"Thanks anyhow, son," I say aloud. "You're not off the hook though. I'm still going to be watching for your signs."

Ten minutes later, I've stopped at a Texaco gas station near my home to refuel. While filling the tank, a thought goes through my mind: I'm not going to watch the dollar amount spin around. Topping off, I replace the gas cap and assess the dollar damage: $21.77.

I chuckle out loud after seeing the number. "Thanks, son," I say. "I'll take that as a sign you're listening."

$$2+1 = \mathbf{3} \quad 7+7 = \mathbf{14}$$

Chapter Ten
My Thoughts Lead the Way

Des Moines, Washington, one month later, 2003

I'm standing on our deck over the garage, waiting on Wanda to return from work. The company she works for, Judson Park Retirement Community is adjacent to our property.

I enjoy watching her stroll leisurely across their well-manicured lawn, between a large variety of plants and flowers, on her way to the house.

On this particular day, as I lean on the railing, my eyes glance down at our Honda Passport in the driveway. My eyes catch sight of the license plate; I stare for a moment, in a trance-like state. It takes a few seconds for the meaning to take a foothold in my brain; my knees almost buckle beneath my weight. I'm looking at a sure sign of Sean being close by and giving another subtle clue.

He's been traveling with us ever since our arrival in Washington. The license plate confirms it! I read it aloud: **"413HNZ."**

413 = **3 & 14**

August, 2003

Wanda and I have been watching John Edward for over a year and a half. The time has finally come for John to bring his seminar tour back to the Emerald City – Seattle.

I'd won a gift certificate in a promotion by a local radio station for a free night stay at the Seattle Red Lion Hotel. I choose to use it on the night John Edward will be in town. It'll make it easier for Wanda, her mother and I to get to the crowded seminar hassle free.

Convention Center, Seattle, Saturday, August 23rd, 2003

Over three thousand people are expected to attend tonight's seminar at 7 p.m.

The waiting line is expected to be long; the doors to the Convention Center are opened at 9:00 a.m., and the line begins to form before the attendant can move out of the way.

The seating arrangement is on a first come first serve basis. I arrive approximately five hours in advance, at 2:00 p.m. I hope to get a decent place in line to have a chance at getting a row of seats close to the front.

Besides Wanda and her mother Fran, my work associate Marilynn and her friend will be joining us on this night. I tell Wanda to take their time getting down to the Center. It's only a few blocks away and easy walking distance from the hotel.

"I'll save a place in line." I said. "Just follow the long procession of people until you find me. Try to be there by 5 to 5:30."

We both have our cell phones in case the ladies get lost. This is a good possibility, especially since there are a lot of stores between the hotel and the Convention Center.

I find my way to the end of the line; all the chairs have been taken by the early morning arrivals. My eyes catch sight of a few straggler chairs at the far end of the waiting arena.

The walk for an elusive chair is about two football fields in length. I ask the lady in front of me if she'll hold my spot in line.

"I'll bring you back a chair to sit on," I negotiate.

During the long waiting period, I begin to talk to the lady in line behind me. She and her husband sitting next to her also lost a son.

Sharing stories about our sons seem to fill the void and pass the time as we sit and wait for the crowd of people to move forward.

Their son's name is Bryan Paul; he died the previous year in November. An enlisted military man, he lost his life in a freak helicopter accident overseas at just 22 years old.

The line begins to move around 5:45 p.m. It'll take a little time to seat the more than 3500 people who've showed up for this seminar.

John Edward turns out to be more spectacular in person. His stage presence and his confidence in his knowledge resonate throughout the room. It's more dramatic being in the audience than on your couch at home and watching on TV; it's also the only way of receiving a visit from a dead relative or friend on this particular night.

As expected, because of the overabundance of people, we and the Abercrombies aren't among the chosen few...

I had a longtime friend from early childhood named Alan. We attended grade school together from the very beginning, and no matter how the school district was divided, we were always together:

Kindergarten and first grade is spent at Browning Elementary, and second grade we attended Lincoln Elementary. Third and fourth grade took us farther away to the Chandler Technical Elementary School, and fifth and sixth grade brought us back to our original starting school at Browning Elementary. We spend our first year of junior high at Willoughby Junior High School.

The streets we lived on are close by in the neighborhood, thus making it easy to get together after school and during various school breaks.

When it comes time for high school, however, we're forced in different directions. My father wants his family back in the school district from which he graduated high school, Mentor High. Mentor High falls within the city limits of Mentor, Ohio; it's also the rival high school of South High in nearby Willoughby, Ohio – the school Alan will be attending in the fall.

The last time I saw Alan is at a house party in 1968; I'd just gotten out of the Marine Corps in early June. Sean is still inside his mother's womb for another month or two.

$$1968 = 1+9+6+8 = 24 \quad 6+8 = 14$$

I think back to my Dad's pictures on the high school football team. He's voted star center his senior year. He also contributes a lot of art drawings to the yearly schoolbook annuals. I can never figure out why he didn't choose a career in art.

Memories of his drawings make me think of my current dilemma with my own son, Travis, and his art expertise left on hold.

Sean graduated high school in 1986. This is the last time he'd see his grandfather alive. Wanda, Rayshal, Travis and I fly back from Pago Pago to Cleveland to attend Sean's graduation ceremony.

$$1986 = 1+9+8+6 = 24 \quad 8+6 - 14$$

One year later, in 1987, my father is fighting cancer. My sister makes an overseas phone call to American Samoa. She tells me the doctor recommends I fly back home if I want to see him alive for the last time.

The flight from Samoa to Cleveland was interminable, but fortunately I make it in time to visit my dad. I stay almost a full week. Each time I enter the room, Dad seems more miserable and agitated as the days pass; I know it's caused by the medicine he's receiving, so I ignore it, even though it hurts.

"How much longer can he remain like this?" I ask the doctor.

"It could be an hour, a day, a week, or months, the doctor admits. "I wish I could tell you more."

I say my good-byes to my dad and the rest of the family. A few hours later, I'm on a flight heading back in the direction of the South Pacific. I arrive in the early morning hours, Pago Pago time.

After only a few hours of sleep, the phone rings; my father has just passed away. I put on my jogging outfit and begin a slow three-mile run to say my good-byes and clear my emotions.

1986 - Last time my father saw Sean
9/23/1919 - 11/13/**1987** - John Wellington Spalding
Age 68 = 6+8 = **14**
1986 = 1+9+8+6 = **24**   **1987** = 1+9+8+7 = **25**
24 & 25 - Radisson Hotel, Portland, Oregon rooms

September 2003
Over the past 35 years, I often wonder what happened to Alan. Many times I would call various cities trying to track him down after receiving a clue from someone with which I'd had a conversation. Unfortunately, every time this always led to a dead end.

I decide to join *classmates.com* this year. It's an internet service that locates classmates, military service friends, and the like.

Alan isn't registered in the school listing; however, a mutual classmate named Ed is listed. Ed was the guest-of-honor at a 1968 party hosted by Alan at his parents' house celebrating Ed's acceptance to the military academy at Annapolis, Maryland.

Following a few emails with Ed, I have Alan's email address, phone number and company name. "Be gentle on the old guy," Ed warns. "You don't want to give him a heart attack after all of these years."

I need a good plan of attack. After **35 years**, while I need to be gentle, I also need to be creative.

My email to Alan contains many hints and clues about our childhood and teen years together. I withhold my name to test his memory skills; after all, Alan and I are both in our late-fifties.

I receive a quick response to my email, and Alan proves to be very good at the game – he retains quite a few memories from early childhood, and some of his personal recollections challenge my own memory.

His second email particularly catches my attention. It provides basic information about his present life: his second wife, Paula

Leo, the mother of his only son and his high school sweetheart, had recently passed months earlier. This leaves Alan to raise his son Toby alone. Toby just turned **14** this year, and Alan's father passed away ten years earlier in **1993.**

Why we make contact after 35 years is a mystery to me. Why his mother decided to clean out some drawers and send him an old childhood photo of us and a few of our friends a few days after my email – who knows? Alan hasn't been in contact with his mother for several weeks.

Even though my number theory is progressing at a faster pace, it still doesn't provide an easy answer to all the situations I encounter. Nevertheless, I feel the answer to many questions and situations will make themselves known in time with Sean's help. Regarding time, our reference is not in the same form as the other side.

Toby **14** years old   Alan's Father dies **1993**
Last contact **35** years - Sean would've been **35** in September 1993

Las Vegas, Nevada, Thursday morning, September 11th, 2003
Our flight left Seattle around 6:05 a.m. The memories of September 11th, 2001 are still on our minds. Wanda and I are seated in the first row of the coach cabin sipping on *Bloody Marys.*

To succumb to the fear that 9-11 brought to the flying public is to allow the terrorists around the world to win. That's something I cannot and will not do!

Wanda and I are celebrating our 25th wedding anniversary. Our celebration is taking place in the neon lights of Las Vegas. Our expenses are prepaid in advance by my employer; unfortunately, I also have to attend my company's conference for managers being held at the *Stratosphere Hotel and Casino* on the far north end of the strip.

Las Vegas, Saturday, September 13, 2003
The company's annual *touchy-feely* course takes place this day. We're divided into separate rooms and groups. Each room has four to five tables with eight or nine managers seated around each.

We're instructed to tell the other managers seated at our table something about ourselves unknown to them. "I belong to Clan Murray and I like wearing a kilt," I announce. I also ask if they are familiar with: *"Crossing Over with John Edward."*

After receiving a positive response, I relate my story and my number theory to those at the table; it takes some time to share the whole story, and between the classroom work and the free time we're allowed, I finally conclude my story by late afternoon. My narrative is received without criticism; if any are skeptical, they keep it to themselves. Before dismissal, one of the managers seated across from me, tells everyone at the table about his drive from Phoenix to Las Vegas a few days earlier.

"There're three of us riding together," he begins. "At some point, the topic of John Edward, or mediums like him, comes up. I tell them, 'I'm still sitting on the fence on my belief. I'd like to talk with someone who's actually had a reading, by a top notch medium, and get their take on it before I make a decision.'"

The table cleared pretty quickly after this confession; everyone was headed in the direction of the closest bar. I head back to my room to get Wanda, so we can begin our own adventure 'on the town.'

Watch What You Wish For

Renton tower, October, 2003

I've gotten use to the various thought messages going through my mind; today is no different. I pull up Suzane's web site, and as it unfolds on the screen, I click on the tab marked "Calendar of Events."

Suzane will be in Seattle November 7th at 7 p.m., and my tickets are ordered as quickly as my fingers can dial. I also make a mental note to let a few of my friends know she's coming to town; a request they made a few months earlier.

I sense Sean is over my shoulder watching and listening when a shiver passes through me. I already feel it will be an eventful night; a night when I'll be surrounded by family, friends – and **witnesses!**

$$11/07/2003 = 1+1+7+2+3 = \mathbf{14}$$

Des Moines, Washington, Wednesday, November 5, 2003

At 3 p.m., I just get home from work and turn on the television to watch the *"Northwest Afternoon,"* a live show popular in Seattle. It has interesting guests each day, as well as a daily update on all the TV soap operas; it's also the same show Suzane Northrop will be on the following day.

During the first intermission, a highlighted performance of Suzane Northrop from a previous appearance is pictured on the screen.

My inner thoughts take control of my movements; walking into the kitchen to the telephone, my fingers flip through the phone book pages purposefully. I'm looking for the number for *KOMO Broadcasting Station Channel 4.*

"Why am I even doing this?" I ask myself. "I don't even know if this is how you get tickets to the show."

My question is answered within seconds. I hear a voice recorded message: "If you're interested in being a guest in our studio audience, please leave your name, phone number, and the date and guest you'd like to have tickets for. If there are seats available, you'll be contacted in advance by telephone."

After following the instructions, I hang up the phone. "Why'd I wait till the last minute to think of this?" I chastise myself.

The same day I ordered tickets for the seminar, Wanda and I agreed to take both Thursday and Friday off, so we can stay at home and watch the show on television. Wanda walks in the front door a little before 5:00 p.m. I decide to keep the phone call to myself; I don't want to hear the famous, "Why didn't you?"

It's about 6:30 p.m. and we just finish eating dinner. The phone rings, and the caller ID reads: *Fisher Broadcasting Company.*

"Hello," I answer.

"I'd like to speak with Dennis Spalding," says a young female sounding voice.

"Speaking," I reply.

She tells me I have two tickets reserved for the 12:00 p.m. to 2:00 p.m. taping tomorrow, Thursday, November 6th. The taping will be in addition to the live broadcast later that day at 3:00 p.m. Suzane has agreed in advance to the double taping.

Writing down her instructions regarding directions to the studio and where to park, she notes, "It sits right across from the Space Needle. Our outside wall has a giant mural of *Ichiro,*" she adds.

For those who don't follow major league baseball, Ichiro Suzuki is one of the stars of the Seattle Mariners. Presently in his second year with the team, he came to the Mariners from the Japanese professional league the previous year, and became an All-Star his rookie year with the Mariners.

I hang up the phone and walk into the living room where Wanda is sitting. "Guess where we're going tomorrow?" I say with a smile.

Chapter Eleven

Lights, Camera, Action...Thank You!

Des Moines, Washington, Thursday morning, November 6, 2003

I toss and turn for most of the night. My brain is bombarded with thought messages. When I awake, I know the next two days of my life are going to be something.

Wanda is sitting by the kitchen counter reading a newspaper when I walk out to get a cup of coffee. I sit down across from her at the dining room table and grab paper and pencil.

"Do you have any idea how much energy is flowing around us today and tomorrow?" I ask.

"Because of Suzane being in town?" she replies.

"Yes, but look at these other numbers!"

I read off Suzane Northrop's number placement in the alphabet. This is something we've gotten use to over the years. I also read off my new discoveries: The street address for KOMO Channel 4 studios, our taping time and the date for tomorrow's seminar.

Suzane = 86 = 8+6 = **14**   Northrop = 124 = **14 & 24**
Taping time 12:00 - 2:00 p.m. = 12+2 = **14**
Address: 4th Ave and John Street
J = 10   **N** = 14   10+14 = **24**   N = **14**
O = 15   **H** = 8   15+8 = 23
23 & 4th Ave =
24- Day of Birth
3- March Month of Death
2+3+4 = **9** September Month of Birth
9 & 3 = **93** Year of Death

I'm reminded of the seminar in Portland, Oregon.

"You said the numbers were real strong a day or so before that seminar, and look what happened," Wanda says.

I stare at the numbers I'd written; I remember sitting in the living room chair during the middle of the night back in late February. I make a note at the top of the paper to log the information in my journal.

"If you get yourself ready early, I'll treat you to breakfast in Seattle before the taping," I offer.

One hour later, we close the front door behind us and exchange a small kiss before backing the car out of the driveway.

Seattle, Washington, KOMO 4 Studios
The lady said to be here by noon. Wanda and I walk through the door a little after 11:00 a.m. The representative at the security desk directs us to the room across the hall.

"Somebody from the *Northwest Afternoon* staff will be down around noon," he said, pointing us in the direction of a large waiting room.

A large, cozy fire is already burning in the two-sided fireplace. We take a seat on the sofa in front of the gas fireplace, and begin watching the television mounted on the wall above the fireplace.

"Do you think they'll mind if I turn to the Channel 5 News?" I smile at Wanda.

"I think not," she replies.

The minutes begin to tick off the clock. The doors around the lobby begin to open and close as people arrive at the station. Some have come alone, while others are in small groups; I wonder how many people this studio will hold.

A voice interrupts my thoughts. "Can everyone please line up at the desk, so I can get you signed in?" says a lady standing behind me. Looking over my shoulder, I see a young blond female attendee in charge of the operation. "We need to give everyone a piece of paper, after checking you off our list, so we can get you through security," she adds.

Once the initial check-in is complete, everyone begins to line up for a security check. The screener ruffles through all handbags before ushering everyone through a small metal detector and into a smaller room in front of an elevator.

Wanda and I take a seat along the glass partition that separates the room from the main buildings' security check-in counter located across the hallway.

After the security check is completed, the girl announces, "I'm sorry for the delay. "They're still getting the studio ready for the audience."

There are only a few people **in the know** who are aware of the extra taping being done this day for Suzane Northrop. On a normal day, the studio crews had another one and a half hours before the taping studio had to be ready for the live broadcast at 3:00 p.m.

I look over my shoulder towards the lobby entrance and notice a couple walking through the main doors. Their faces look very familiar; I tap Wanda on the shoulder.

"Suzane and her book representative are checking in," I said.

The two ladies seated in front of us had stopped talking for a moment. As a courtesy, I lean forward and tell them Suzane is off to their right checking in at the desk.

"Who's Suzane Northrop?" asks the lady closest to the glass partition.

"**Duh!**" I think to myself. "She's the medium for the guest spot today," I inform.

"Somebody told me Sylvia Browne is coming to town; I was hoping it was her today," she replies.

"Sylvia is very good, but **Suzane offers a different perspective**," I reply exuberantly. "Suzane is like John Edward, but her style is a little different."

The lady eyes Suzane up and down. "She doesn't look like she can be very good," she says disapprovingly. "Besides, I think John Edward is too generalized. Most of what he validates can fit anybody."

That's it, I've heard enough! Wanda knows something is coming; my agitation in the seat is a sure giveaway.

"How many times have you seen John Edward?" I counter.

"I've only seen the show once," she replies.

"I think you'd better watch the show a few more times before you make statements like that," I say. "There's nothing generalized about him."

The lady decides to end our little confrontation, and continues the discussion with her friend I interrupted earlier. Glancing over at Wanda, I roll my eyes.

"Must be from Bellevue and got excited over the free tickets to the taping," I whisper in her ear.

"They're ready for us upstairs," the lady in charge announces.

Everyone stands up as the wide elevator doors open in front of us. As we load onto the elevator, I'm thinking about the next hour that's approaching rather quickly; I imagine others are too – except for the lady from Bellevue – she's still in deep conversation with her friend.

The crowd gathers outside the studio door after exiting the elevator. An audience representative escorts a few at a time into the studio for seating. Each time her head pops out the door, she consults a list on her clipboard and calls out a few names. When Wanda and mine are called, we are directed to the far side of the studio, where we take a seat at the very top. I do a quick head count after everyone is seated. I know from previous experience the less the better.

"There aren't even 50 people in here," I whisper to Wanda. The studio looks a lot bigger on TV.

The audience representative introduces the various television crew members and stage hands. She describes their specific duties and what to expect during the taping; she also explains what they expect from the audience members.

It's time for the audience to practice. A crew member's hand held high in the air means to sit upright in your seat and smile; no gum chewing, please. When the fist opens and the fingers begin to wave, that means its time to applaud; you can yell, shout, or even whistle if you want.

"When I bring my hand down slowly, please start to let up on your applause and the extra noise," she instructs. "Now let's practice a few times to prepare and make sure we've got it down right for the cameras."

Suzane enters to a loud response from the audience on cue (except for the lady from Bellevue); the camera lights come on and the taping is underway.

Even though it's not a live show, the program is stopped at various times for commercial breaks. The producer explains how the taping is used during an **emergency no show** by other guests.

"We need something live in the can to keep the show going at all costs," he says.

During a break midway through the readings, the co-hosts and a few crew members join Suzane on stage. A voice overhead (actually coming from the director's booth outside the studio) tells the crew and the co-hosts: "Look at her shoes! This happened the last time she was here."

The audience focuses their attention on center stage, where Suzane is standing surrounded by various crew members. Her shoes are the only ones with carpet fiber stuck around the side of each shoe. It's obvious to the naked eye she creates a lot of energy during the readings.

"I wonder what her carpets look like at home?" jokes the voice from above.

As the commercial break approaches an end, the crew prepares the audience and we respond as instructed. Suzane continues the readings, and the television cameras focus in on the individual receiving the reading.

The station has an agenda. They're looking for that special camera shot; the emotional reaction from an audience member who's just received a message from a loved one. Suzane, as we know, can only follow the script provided to her by the cast on the other side.

Before we know it, much to our disappointment the taping is over and the credits are about to roll across the screen. The telephone resting on the producer's podium rings.

"Okay, everybody, listen up," he instructs after hanging up the phone. "The director wants another six minutes of readings put on film."

Most of the segments taped are in six-minute increments. When the director doesn't like what he taped in one of the segments, or the reaction by a specific audience member is too blasé, he'll order more taping in hopes of receiving a better reaction the next time.

"Where do you want me to stand?" asks Elisa, one of the co-hosts.

She's directed toward the top of the stairs in our vicinity; the other co-host, Kent Phillips, proceeds to the top of the stairs on the opposite side. The director decides to begin with Elisa, and the stage hand next to the camera man cues Elisa: five...four...three...two...one – and his finger points in her direction. The red light on the camera comes on, and the taping continues once again.

"Suzane, are you receiving any more vibrations or energies in these final minutes?" she asks.

"I've got two energies coming through," Suzane replies.

The first energy goes to a lady seated below and to our right. She's sitting next to the lady and her friend from Bellevue. Within seconds, Elisa is standing next to the woman. A microphone is held up close to her face so the studio and television audiences can hear every word.

Once that reading is over, Suzane begins to pace around the stage. "This next energy is very, very strong and powerful," she informs the audience. "**Sean!**"

A lady seated in front of Wanda and I calls out to Suzane: "My name is Shawna," she offers. Suzane's head shakes back and forth. "This is a very strong **male** energy," she advises.

I raise my hand. "I have a son, Sean!" I reply. Elisa grabs my arm to have me stand up for the camera and the studio audience.

"Why would he be showing me a lot of airplanes?" she asks.

"I'm an air traffic controller," I respond.

"That would explain it," she acknowledges. "I'm definitely with you."

I glance back at Wanda. I can't believe its actually taking place again. Even when you sense it can happen, you're still caught by surprise when it actually does.

"Are you aware he hangs out around the airport quite a lot?" she asks.

I think about all of the number 14's surrounding my tower on a daily basis. "Yes," I agree. "I'm quite aware of the number connection he has there."

"Are you still connected with his mother?" she asks, her eyes focusing in my direction.

"We're divorced," I answer.

Her response is quick. "But she's aware of what's going on?"

I quickly review the past year: My elation in seeing our story in print, along with everything else that happened during the year. I remember Sean's strong influence on my picking up the phone after 10 long years to call his mother. I make a mental note to call Pat after the seminar, even though I still remember Rob's negativity the last time we talked.

"She's been brought up to date," I confess. "In part from a reading I received from you over the radio, and the paragraphs in your book."

This last reply catches the ear of Elisa. "You've had a reading before this one?" she asks.

"Yes," I reply, trying to stay focused on Suzane.

"Well, you've had your fair share of readings, I'd say," she comments.

My thoughts quickly defend from this imagined attack. I can't control the spirit world; they come across whenever and to whomever they want. I don't remember quotas on readings.

Whenever the station has a psychic or medium for a guest, the audience members and television viewers have a habit of complaining to the television station about not receiving a reading, or the readings in general. They say some people seem to occupy too much of the station's allowed time.

"I'm there for anyone I know who has crossed over – this includes my son!" I say to Elisa. "If someone has a message to get to a loved one, I'll be happy to receive it and pass it along."

Suzane senses my defensive posture, and quickly regains control of the situation. "He's here to thank you for making those connections with his mother and keeping her informed," she relays.

I thank Suzane and sit back down in my seat, but my mind does a fast rewind and replay.

The signal is given to end the readings. Elisa and Kent say their final thoughts and good-byes to the viewing audience. The broadcast is over as quickly as it began.

Wanda and I are the last to leave the room. "That was interesting!" I say to Wanda.

"You said this morning there's high energy around us," Wanda replies.

The elevator is already loaded, and we're the last to squeeze in. "I'll try to get Suzane's website address for you downstairs," the young lady in charge is saying to a lady in the far back.

Having spent many hours on Suzane's site, I reply automatically, "Its www.theseance.com."

We arrive back at the house around 3:00 p.m. I'm anxious to let Sean's mom know about the message I received at the studio. I figure Alabama is about two to three hours ahead of Pacific time; hopefully, I'm not catching them at dinner and they think I'm one of those intrusive telemarketers.

As I hear the phone ringing on the other end, I think back to February when I called Pat the morning after the seminar in

Portland to share an update on Suzane's revelations. I shared a few things with her husband Rob before talking with her; that seemed to change the mood of our conversation compared to our discussion three days earlier.

Rob answers the phone, "Hello." I recognize his voice.

"Rob," I reply. "This is Dennis; can I please speak to Pat for a moment."

A few seconds later I recognize Pat's distinctive accent. "This is Pat," she answers.

"Pat, this is Dennis," I begin. "I've got a little more information from Sean to tell you..."

Before I can finish the sentence she's already begun talking. "Would you please do me a favor and don't call anymore in regards to this topic," she demanded before I hear a loud click; she'd hung up on me.

Stunned, I glance at the receiver held in my left hand. The dial tone has been replaced with the recording, "If you wish to make a call please hang up and..."

"Wanda!" I call out. "You're not going to believe this.

Later that night, my last thought before drifting off to sleep is wondering what tomorrow, November 7, 2004, has in store for the Spalding's.

$$11/07/2003 = 1+1+7+2+3 = \mathbf{14}$$

Part Two – My Journey Continues

Chapter Twelve
Yes! He's Showing Me Numbers!

Des Moines, Washington, Friday, November 7, 2003

I like to be early in things I do and places I go, and today is no exception. The seminar doesn't start till 7 p.m., but I convince Wanda to be ready early for lunch in Seattle. If she'll agree, I also offer the possibility of a little window shopping in advance, although there'll be very little actual buying.

Seattle, Renaissance Hotel 11:00 a.m.

The seminar is going to be held at the Renaissance Hotel, and we park in their underground lot. Before getting any lunch and doing our window shopping, I decide to check out the room where the seminar will be held later this evening.

I look inside the conference room and see about 50 to 60 chairs set up. "Alright!" I shout. "This is bad for Suzane, but it's good for the audience and us," I tell Wanda.

Once again, this means less DP's show up on the other side, trying to out shout each other for recognition from Suzane.

We eat in the hotel lounge, and during lunch we ask the hostess for the dinner menu. Marilynn and Kathy, the Clan Murray commissioner, are meeting us for dinner before the seminar around 5 p.m.

Unfortunately the hotel café is closed on Friday nights, and the Italian Restaurant housed on the top floor is way overpriced; Wanda and I both agree the lounge will be the most convenient place.

After lunch, we stroll down the sidewalk on our window shopping adventure. About one block into our walk, I notice a lady approaching who passes off to our right. Wanda and I stop, look at each other and comment in unison: "Wasn't that Suzane who just passed by?"

We both turn around to see the lady stopping at the next corner; she pauses for a moment to look back in our direction, before continuing on to her destination.

"If that's her, maybe she's trying to figure out where she's seen us? I say. "I must've left a lasting impression on her at the TV studio yesterday."

Later, Wanda held true to her promise and the window shopping adventure is a success. I treat her to a cocktail at the Sheraton Hotel lounge before heading back up the street to meet Kathy and Marilynn at the Renaissance Hotel lounge.

When we return to the Renaissance Hotel about 4:15, I notice Kathy is already seated at the bar. We chat about our dinner options before taking a table in the lounge and wait for Marilynn to show.

Rayshal's husband John is attending a three-day teachers' conference down the street at the Sheraton Hotel. John spent the previous night at our house because the long drive back to Olympia after each day's meetings seemed to be a waste of time and money.

The night before the seminar John told us he'd like to attend; I was very much surprised, as I wrote earlier, John is one of my number theories worst critics. The fact he'd even want to attend something of this nature gives me a sense of accomplishment, and I enthusiastically welcome his company.

Earlier I offered to pick up John's ticket so he could leave his school conference at the scheduled time without having to rush only to stand in line. Marilynn arrives a few minutes late. She didn't read my driving directions until the last minute and took a wrong exit off Interstate 5. After a brief exchange of amenities, I ask the waitress for the menus.

We're in no rush to get a good seat because of the small turnout expected. After ordering the meals I excuse myself for a few minutes. "I'm going to run upstairs and get John's ticket and a book for Travis," I explain.

When I walk into the conference room, I notice Ira the *Jodere Publishing Company* representative on one side of the room retrieving program supplies from a box.

"Can I help you?" he asks.

"I want to get a ticket for my son-in-law and a book."

Making his way across the room, he stops partway; his eyes wrinkle in thought and his head tips slightly to the side.

"Isn't your name, Dennis?" he asks.

"Yes," I respond, a small grin creeping across my face.

"You've got a son, Sean, who passed away?" he asks rhetorically.

"Yes," I reply again.

"You were also at the taping yesterday at the studio, right?" he asks.

"Yes I was."

"Aren't you also the one who came to Portland to thank Suzane for something in her book, and you had a lot of numbers written down to show her?"

"That's me," I say pleasantly.

He then relates how he saw me on the television monitor back stage yesterday, when I received my reading from Suzane. "Do you know who that last person is you just finished reading?" he asks her.

"No," Suzane replies. Like most mediums of her caliber, they're so wired during the sessions, they're lucky to remember their own names afterward.

After a brief refresher course about the Portland seminar, she begins to recall a few fragments of what took place.

By now, people are starting to arrive early for the seminar. They begin to line up behind me, and I notice John is part of the crowd. I excuse myself so Ira can take care of business, and go back downstairs to join the ladies and finish my meal.

I'm so wired after my conversation with Ira, I realize I had forgotten about John's ticket and Travis' book. I ask John to take care of it. "I'll pay you back later," I said.

Looking back on that now, I didn't think to ask if he was hungry and if he wanted to join us for dinner downstairs. "Try to save seats in the last row for five of us," I instruct John as I strode towards the elevator.

Downstairs, I rejoin our dinner gathering and ask, "Guess what just happened upstairs?"

After relaying the story, I glance at my watch. I didn't realize how long I'd been gone. I suggest the ladies join John upstairs, while I finish woofing down my meal in a manly manner, subtly suggesting they may not want to witness that experience.

"Good idea," Kathy agrees. "I'd rather not watch given a choice." The other two women agree with Kathy in unison – a bit quickly, I noted.

"Since you ladies are being so nice to me, I'll take care of the check and see you upstairs," I offer.

Arriving upstairs a few minutes later, I see that the women had already found John and the seats he reserved in the last row. We have about 15 minutes before the program begins.

A short time later, after Ira shares with the gathering what to expect and some background on Suzane's accomplishments and achievements, he announces, "Ladies and gentlemen, please give a warm welcome to Suzane Northrop!"

Suzane enters the room behind us to a loud ovation by the small crowd. She makes her way down the center aisle to the stage. Before addressing the audience, she arranges her bottles of water on a table next to a single, high seat chair.

Though the seminar is similar to the previous ones, I still manage to learn certain things; questions from the audience will always take the seminar in a different direction.

The meditation portion is about to start. This meditation is designed to help clear our minds of **negative energy** so we can become more receptive to any visits by family, friends or relatives.

Your mind visualizes the seven **Chakra** energy points in the body, and their related colors, as you rise on your journey to a sacred place and a possible meeting with a loved one, friend or your own spirit guide.

The seven energy points start at the base of the spine, the root chakra, and proceed upward to the top of the head, or the crown chakra. The colors normally follow a set pattern used by most mediums.

The root color is always red. The solar plexus is orange and the spleen is yellow. The fourth point is the heart and the color of green. The throat area is blue. The area between your eyes is known as the *third eye* – it's a dark purple, and the final point is the violet-colored crown chakra.

All mediums have their own personal mental journey and place to describe to the audience. It takes full concentration, effort and a positive belief in the process to reach the benefits of this journey.

Not everyone is able to make contact with someone the very first time. Nevertheless, Marilynn is able to see her grandparents. She wrote their names on a sheet of paper before the meditation took place.

Once the readings begin, Suzane peppers the audience with rapid-fire questions. "Why's he showing me a lot of helicopters?" Suzane asks.

Nobody in the audience is acknowledging at this point.

"He's in the military or police force," she adds. "I know this – he's showing me a uniform with stripes on the sleeve." She takes her right arm and motions to her left shoulder; an area where military type insignias are normally worn.

One person raises their hand to offer a vague validation to what Suzane is describing.

I rack my brain for any information dealing with helicopters, or any military buddies that have long passed; nothing comes to mind – nothing to make me feel the message is for me.

"He's overseas," she continues. "I know this when I see land masses divided by water."

A family on the opposite side of the room believes the person coming through is actually for them and not the previous lady.

"I'm hearing the name, Paul," Suzane relays to the audience.

My mind thinks about my Aunt Joanne and my step-uncle Paul. I never heard anything about helicopters in his past; I only knew about his job as a chemical engineer at the plant my aunt use to work for.

I've never heard back from my cousin Jim whether Uncle Paul is still alive or not. I went to visit him once, after the death of my aunt, but that was many years ago.

Aunt Joanne is my mother's older sister. We'd been in one of those family squabbles over a money issue that never really resolved itself prior to her passing about a year or so after I married Wanda. Most of the money had been paid back; unfortunately, it wasn't to Aunt Joanne's liking, and things were said on both sides that shouldn't have been.

After I learned my aunt had become quite ill, I went to visit her in the hospital. I don't think we really settled our differences; nevertheless, I believe she's in a much better place where she's able to drop any of the anger she held against me. I know I've dropped any anger and resentment against her.

In time, I'm certain we'll both come to some sort of resolution where we can face one another once again; she'll stop by one of the seminars I'm attending and say hello.

Even though Suzane accepts a **variety of validations** to the helicopter issue, it still registers in my mind that these validations didn't come from **one particular family.** I can understand this if we had hundreds of people in the room, but when only 45 people are present, it doesn't make much sense.

Suzane continues walking briskly around the room connecting with different families. After another thirty minutes or so, her pacing stops and she stands at the front of the room. Holding her right hand by her forehead, she begins shaking her head from side to side, her eyes narrowing at the brow.

"I'm not going through this again...am I?" she questions aloud. She begins to walk down the center aisle. "I'm seeing those darn helicopters again!"

A new family adds their validation to the mix already on the floor, after hearing the additional clues Suzane has to offer. Because no one else in the audience raises their hand to acknowledge the message, Suzane can only agree with the validation and continue on with more readings for the audience.

After pacing back and forth along the center aisle, she finally stops at the front of the room to look out into the audience; her head moves slowly from side to side.

"Let me see if I have any more dead people left in the room," she chides. "Maybe I can clear the room tonight and you'll all owe me bottles of wine," she adds with a smile and a laugh.

Her eyes look toward a lady in the second row of our section. The message from the other side seems to bring relief and comfort to this woman.

After the message is delivered, Suzane looks in our direction. Her right hand is slowly stroking her lower jaw.

"I've got a strong male energy pacing back and forth behind this last row of chairs!" she states, her arm and finger pointing in our direction. "Has anyone back there lost a son?"

I raise my hand; I can't believe it's happening two days in a row, even though I knew Thursday morning the numbers were very strong for these two seminars. "I have," I said.

"Would he know everyone seated with you in that row?" she asks.

My mind thinks quickly – John is married to Rayshal – yes! Marilynn has heard many of my stories while working in the tower – yes! Kathy has heard several stories about him and Suzane, in fact, is one of the reasons she came – yes! Wanda goes without saying – yes! We all came to the seminar as a group; in the psychic world we're connected like a family – so the answer is yes!

"Yes!" I answer adamantly.

"Is his mother with you?" she asks.

I motion in Wanda's direction. "This is his step-mother."

Suzane turns her attention to Wanda. "Do you know he's come to visit you before?" she informs rhetorically.

During the start of our reading, Ira placed a microphone in my hand. This helps the audience members seated around the room to hear what the person says in response to Suzane's questions. I hold the microphone up close to Wanda as she responds.

"Yes," she replies. She told me later her thoughts went back to our living room when the number 29 appeared on the television. Her mind also tries to remember other visits that might've taken place.

"This is a very busy boy!" Suzane states. "He's telling me Sean, or Shane?"

"His name is Sean," I reply.

She then forwards an unusual message. "He likes his name," she says.

I can't think of anything else to say to the validation but, "That's why we gave it to him." The audience laughs.

"Why's he telling me…**numbers**?" she asks.

I can't believe I'm hearing a validation to my numbers theory! I look around a room full of strangers; my worst critic and skeptic sits two seats to my right. Sean must feel the timing is right to bring this out: a validation for his father, from the other side, to a process occurring on this side.

I begin shaking in my chair; my arms stiffen, and I feel my body hairs rise up, followed by the goose bumps. I've been trying to tell people this for years, and now in front of an audience, **my son is validating my story!**

"You really have me shaking now," I confide to Suzane in front of the audience. "I've had this theory for some time on how my son is communicating with me through numbers. It starts through a reading I received from you on a radio program."

My body starts trembling. I remember a similar experience after I discovered the numbers for Sean's birth and death, a few days after my reading with Suzane over the radio.

I can feel Wanda clenching my right arm. I finish my validation. "There's also a reference to this in your latest book. These numbers have taken me on a journey; a long journey!" I exclaim. "In fact, they led me to the television studios yesterday, where you also made a connection with him…and now this!"

Thanks to Sean, the door is kicked wide open. This isn't the time to stop any revelations from coming out. I've taken the stage away from Suzane, if only for a moment, so I need to use this time wisely.

"The connection with my son, and the journey I'm on, goes through you!" I state passionately. "You're a **catalyst** to everything that's happened, and will continue to happen. If our story is to be told, then it will have to come through you, or with your help. The ball seems to be in your court for now. My son and I will just have to sit back and wait – for the moment."

Suzane stands frozen at the front of the room. She can only smile, shake her head and shrug her shoulders; her arms and hands are uplifted in a gesturing motion – speechless.

Finally, after a few moments, she regains her composure. "This boy is very persistent!" she exclaims. Her right finger is held up to her right temple in the form of a gun to her head. "I'm not going to take him home with me tonight; he's going home with you!"

"He's coming home with me, but don't forget – we'll both be waiting," I warn.

The night's final validation **from the other side** surprises all of us seated in the back row. "Why's he showing me…**a book?**" Suzane asks.

I explain to her and the audience how I've kept a journal over the years, because of the numerous messages and clues I'd been receiving.

"I made this journal into a story. It's a memorial, a tribute to him, as well as to all the other friends and relatives referenced in the story that've been with me on this journey from the beginning," I state proudly. "It's a story worth reading – and a story worth telling; especially after tonight's revelations."

Suzane decides the seminar should end on this note; I couldn't agree more. Sean has boldly stepped forward from the other side where **he lives**, to promote a book on this side where **I live.**

I can only hope the book he's showing Suzane is an already **published edition** of our story.

To Date: 11/7/2003
7 Seminars attended: 4 Seminars no readings / 3 Seminars with a reading
7+4+3 = **14**
11/7/2003 = 1+1+7+2+3 =
14

Chapter Thirteen

My First Mission

Seattle, Renaissance Hotel conference room, Friday night 9:40 p.m.

Wanda and I wait in line after the seminar to get the book I bought for Travis autographed. He'd never let us forget it if the book arrived without a signature.

Suzane looks up as we approach the table. I place a tablet down on the table in front of her. "I just want to show you a few of the clues that led me to the television studios yesterday," I said.

I tell her about my phone call to Sean's mother after the television reading; the fact she's now **close minded** and cut off all phone conversation with me.

"You can't do any more than that," she replies. "You've honored the process by trying."

Before leaving the table, Wanda explains how Sean and I had always been in contact with one another. If we couldn't do it in person, we'd use the phone or write letters and postcards.

"They communicated all the time back then," she tells Suzane. "I guess there's no reason they shouldn't stay in contact with each other now."

"Linda has all of my phone and email contacts if you need to get hold of me," I tell Suzane. "I'm also keeping track of everything that's happening right up to this seminar in my journal."

"Good idea," Suzane agrees, shaking my hand as we say good-bye. Before leaving the table, I apologize for the delay to the people waiting in line behind me.

"That's okay," they cry out in unison, inching closer to the desk. "We're just interested in what you and Suzane had to say to each other."

Suzane's assistant Linda and I have been in email contact for some time. My friends are impressed how quickly an email response is generated out of her office.

I try to keep her informed on important events in my life that relate to communication from Sean. In fact, she's my go-between in trying to make Suzane aware of her importance to the story between my son and me. I've never mentioned Sean's name to Linda; I've only referenced him as my son.

John is standing in the hallway outside the conference room. I had said my good-byes to Kathy and Marilynn before heading into the book signing line.

Since John is spending one more night at the house, Wanda will ride home with him. I'll drive to Sea-Tac (Seattle-Tacoma) Airport for my midnight shift taking weather observations.

The three of us excitedly discuss the seminar on our way down the elevator to the parking garage below.

Seattle, Washington, Sea-Tac airport, later that night.

As I near the top of the final flight of stairs by the weather observer's office, I realize I'm still wired from the seminar. I receive my briefing from the observer on duty.

After sitting down, I pull out my notes from the seminar, along with files, notes and memos from the past few years regarding my studies in the afterlife.

The folder contains information on various mediums, and fell open to the John Edward section. My eyes transfix on a note attached at the top: an address and e-mail address for the Abercrombie's. Written across the top in bold letters is their son's name: **Bryan Paul** age 22.

A flash jolts my brain! I realize I forgot to transfer Bryan Paul's name to my list of family, friends and relatives that have passed on; the list I use during my meditations.

During the seminar, Suzane had mentioned the name **Paul** during the segment about helicopters.

"Son-of-a-bitch!" I yell out aloud. "It was you trying to come through all the time."

My thoughts catapult back a few days, to a conversation I had with Marilynn in the tower cab one morning.

"Every time I think about your street address, the name ***Abercrombie*** *comes to mind," I told her. "I know that isn't it, but it makes me start to think about the couple I met at the John Edward seminar while waiting in line."*

"Have you talked with them recently?" Marilynn asked.

"I'm thinking of calling or emailing them next week, just to see how they're getting along.

Bryan Paul knew, on this particular day, I'd be a good candidate to come to with his message on Friday. I become totally apologetic.

"I'll call your parents in the morning and tell them the story," I say to him aloud.

I sit back and try to recall everything said at the seminar regarding the reading on helicopters. I wonder if more validations might've been given if I'd realized the message was for me.

Sea-Tac weather office, Saturday morning, November 8, 2003

The answering machine asks for a name and number. "My name is Dennis Spalding, I met you both at the John Edward semin –" I begin before a male voice answers.

"Hello," he says. "This is Pete. I was just trying to figure out who's calling by the caller I.D."

"Sorry to bother you so early, Pete," I said. "Is your wife Diane there by chance?"

"She's gone for the day," he replied. "Can I help?"

I gather my notes together and sit back in my chair to get comfortable. "If you'll give me a few minutes of your time," I begin. "I've got a story I'd like to tell you."

We talk for almost thirty minutes. I let him know I believe in my heart it was his son coming through with a message for the two of them. "If I'd realized it was him at the time, I think there would've been more information given out," I confide. "It won't happen again! I'll be ready for him next time."

Pete tells a story that's hard to get out of my mind. Their son loved to help his Dad with repairs around the house. He'd work right next to his Dad no matter what the chore entailed.

One day, after his son was killed, the roof needed to be repaired. During a break, Pete remained up on the roof looking out over the surrounding area. A little bird joined him and sat right by his side the whole time.

The meaning of this incident wasn't clear to Pete until the next day. Once again, the little bird joined him on the roof. This continued until the completion of the repairs a day or so later.

When I think about this story I have to remember Sean's mom and her friend at Sean's grave site – **the blue butterfly**.

After listening to a few updates and stories that Pete wanted to share, the call ends. I hang up the phone and sit back in my chair. I look out at the morning sky through the window.

"This feels good," I think to myself. "I've honored the process like I said I would do."

Glancing at the clock on the wall, I see that it's almost 9 a.m.; my shift is about over. I reflect back again on the phone call to the Abercrombie's. "That's my first try on being a messenger," I think. "I'll loosen up a bit more the next time my services are called upon."

Renton airport tower, Monday, November 10, 2003
The alarm goes off early this morning. My time spent in the Marine Corps has etched the meaning of this date in my mind forever; my prayers and thoughts go out to those present and past members of this exclusive club: Happy Birthday! Semper Fi!

I'm hoping to get to the tower early, while Marilynn is still there cleaning, to discuss her thoughts on Suzane's seminar Friday night.

The tower doesn't open until 7:00 a.m. I walk through the door at 5:45 a.m. Marilynn normally arrives a few minutes before six.

We spend about an hour in discussion and note comparing. "The three of you are like a **triangle of energy**," she says, describing the connection between Sean, Suzane and myself.

"Wow!" I interrupt. "Can I use that analogy in my story? In fact, I've got an email going to Linda this morning about the seminar; I'll use it then as well."

"Sure," Marilynn agrees. "I don't think Suzane really knows **how important she really is** to the whole story."

I begin to talk about other portions of the seminar. "Wanda thought she saw Suzane glance over at our section several times during the seminar, as if she knew or saw Sean pacing back and forth waiting."

"I noticed that too," Marilynn agrees. "I was thinking about it over the weekend."

She continues to express her impression of Sean's message. "It was so powerful; along with the effect it had on you, it **had to be delivered** at the very end of the seminar," she marveled. "If his message had come during the middle, I feel the emotion of your response might've overshadowed the effect of other messages that would've been given out toward the end."

Sean had always been a caring and courteous person. He knew the reaction I would have to his message, and the effect it would have on the rest of the audience; he chose to patiently wait until the end of the seminar to deliver this very important validation to his father, as well as the surprise presentation of a **future event**.

"I'm also thinking about my critics," I confess. "Will they say, 'Suzane already knew about parts of my story'? She knew I was in the audience, because she **possibly recognized me** from the previous day, or her assistant Ira was observed pointing in the direction of our group during a conversation at break time."

"No!" Marilynn states adamantly. "I didn't get that feeling at all."

If I even for a moment believed the possibility of my concern on what the critics might say or think, I'd have to ask the question: **"Why?"** Why would a medium risk their reputation by giving a false reading to appease an audience member; a person whose story of which they're partially aware but don't really know in detail, or for that matter, don't know the individual on a personal level?

Furthermore, if that **were the case**, then every reading she'd ever performed throughout her career spanning 25 years would come under scrutiny.

The weather is miserable the rest of the morning, and there are visible signs that winter is quickly approaching. The airplanes are not flying. I sit at the computer and draft an email to Linda.

I choose to make the subject matter: **Dennis-high energy in Seattle.** "This should capture her attention from the other thousand emails she receives daily," I think.

I mention my theory on the helicopter mix-up at the seminar, as well as my phone call to the Abercrombies the next day. I relate various issues about my reading at the television studio during the additional six minute segment, along with my success at Friday's seminar; the joy I feel after having my son boldly validate my numbers theory in front of an audience, Suzane, and one of my critics.

Before I click the send button, I remember to inform her of the new analogy representing Sean, Suzane and myself – the triangle of energy as Marilynn calls it.

"If this symbol representing the bond between the three of us doesn't stay in Suzane's mind, I don't know what will," I mumble aloud.

She has to realize some day how important this story is, and how important she is to the story.

Des Moines, Tuesday, November 11, 2003
Travis and I are standing in the kitchen talking when the phone rings. My sister Diane from Cleveland is on the other end.

"What's going on?" I inquire.

"Uncle Bill just passed away," she informs me. "The funeral is on Thursday, the thirteenth. That's the same day that Dad died."

I hang up the phone and tell Travis the bad news.

"Are you going to fly back for the funeral?" he asks.

"I can't," I reply regrettably. "I've got two jobs to work and nobody to cover for me. Besides, it's in two days!"

I couldn't stop remembering how Uncle Bill said he wanted me to write **his eulogy** after I left the podium at Jack's funeral in May 2002. Uncle Bill had enjoyed the eulogy a lot, despite the silent reactions from the funeral staff over its duration.

Unfortunately, because of the timing of Uncle Bill's departure, I'll have to say my goodbyes in my prayers.

Once Wanda arrives home from work I pass on the bad news. We spend the rest of the night thinking about Uncle Bill, and the joy and meaning he brought into our lives.

I remember the conversation he and I had in his dining room the day after my brother's funeral concerning my belief in the afterlife...

"My first seminar is coming up next month with Suzane Northrop," I said. "I'll let you and Aunt Alby know if anything happens."

*He begins to tell me a touching story, about a dream he had concerning his grandson, who was confined to a wheel chair for most of his life. He died at the age of **fourteen.***

"It was so real to me, Denny," he expresses. "He didn't need his wheel chair and his pain was gone."

Before leaving his house, we sat in the living room and enjoyed a cocktail with him and Aunt Alby. After a personal request from

117

Wanda, my sister Diane and me, we're serenaded by his great tenor voice at the young age of eighty...

I'm sure Sean and my Dad, my uncle's older brother, are there to meet him at his crossover point in the next life. The numbers are strong to back this belief.

11/**11**/2003 Uncle Bill dies
11/**13**/1987 My Dad dies
11+13 = **24** Sean's birth day
11/**13**/2003 Uncle Bill **will be** buried
11/13/2003 = **16** year anniversary of Dad's death
13+16 = **29** Sean's T.V. visit/Roulette number

Des Moines, Thursday, November 13, 2003
Most of the day is spent thinking about Uncle Bill being buried, as well as memories involving my father.

I'm in the living room watching television. I hear my dad at the front door, coming home after work. I'm about five or six. I run to the door to say hello! He's wearing a loose fitting fall coat. Concealed inside this coat is a small, black puppy with little white markings. My brother and I name him Wags.

During a break in the television program, Wanda looks over at me and asks, "Why do you think Sean would come across at the seminar to tell you '**he likes his name**?' Isn't that an odd validation for someone to come across with?"

"I guess," I respond hesitatingly. "That's why I told Suzane what I did; I couldn't think of anything else to say."

"But think about it!" she presses. "Why would he say that?"

It only takes a few seconds for the answer to hit me. I jump up from the chair and grab a piece of paper and pencil.

"What are you doing?" Wanda asks.

"This whole story is about my numbers theory," I reply. "I never thought to run Sean's **full name**, or my name for that matter, in their numerical alphabet letter placement."

Once the numbers are paired against the appropriate letters, I can't believe what I'm seeing. I recheck the numbers to make sure I did it correctly.

I ask Wanda to stand behind me and read over my shoulder as I explain what the letters and numbers mean.

$$Sean = 39 \quad Christopher = 139 \quad Spalding = 82$$
$$Dennis = 65 \quad Lee = 22 \quad Spalding = 82$$
$$39 = \mathbf{3 \ \& \ 93} \quad 139 = 1+3+9 = 13 = 1+3 = \mathbf{4} \quad 82 = 8+2 = 10 = 1+0 =$$
$$\mathbf{1}$$
$$65 = 6+5 = 11 = 1+1 = \mathbf{2} \quad 22 = 2+2 = \mathbf{4} \quad 82 = 8+2 = 10 = 1+0 = \mathbf{1}$$

"The next step is to add the **triangle of energy**, representing Sean, Suzane and myself," I explain.

Wanda looks on as the triangle is beginning to take shape. The meaning hasn't come to her yet.

"Sean's entire date of death is represented in his name," I explain. "If you read my name total, from left to right, the first two numbers represent the day he was born. If you read it from right to left, the first two numbers represent the day he died."

I also add Suzane's numbers from my previous findings

$$Suzane = 86 = 8+6 = \mathbf{14} \quad Northrop = 124 = 1 / 2 / 4 = \mathbf{14 \ \& \ 24}$$

Her name carries a double fourteen. I use only her last name on the energy triangle. What I don't expect, upon completion, is the numbers for my name and Suzane's name to both total seven.

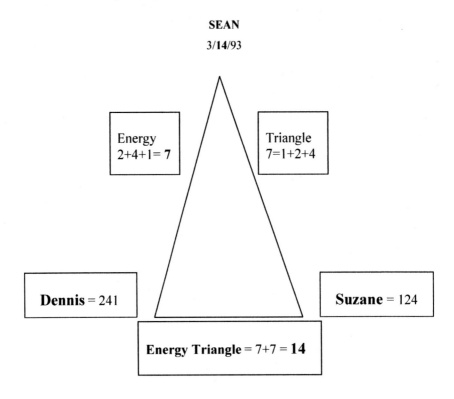

SEAN
3/14/93

Energy
2+4+1= **7**

Triangle
7=1+2+4

Dennis = 241

Suzane = 124

Energy Triangle = 7+7 = **14**

The energy triangle seems to prove my theory involving the vibrancy between the three of us. It shows why Sean led me to Suzane in the first place.

What I have to do now is convince Suzane there's an energy bond between the three of us, a bond so strong it's created a story that needs to be told – a story that will eventually be told with or without her help.

My son showed her a part of our future. He held up a book for her to see clearly, and for her to comment about. I might've misinterpreted the meaning of this message. It's possible the meaning is: **this story will be published and told one day in the future.**

Because Suzane has been such a strong influence during this whole journey, I just assumed my son meant **she's the one** to help get the story published.

Within our frame of reference, time is not the same on the other side. The future will continue to take care of itself. I, on the other hand, will keep moving along with our story, continually updating wherever and whenever my feelings and senses lead me to do so.

Eventually it should take care of itself, no matter who helps out in getting it told to the world. With my son guiding me each day over my shoulder, I know the communication and adventures are going to continue for the rest of my life. I just have to concentrate on my purpose in this life: **to use our story to help others.**

Chapter Fourteen
A Friend in Need...A Book to Read

Renton tower, Monday, November 17, 2003

I arrive at the tower a few minutes early. The door closes behind me as Marilynn is driving into the parking lot. I take care of a few details in my office before proceeding up to the tower cab.

Upon Marilynn's arrival we exchange a few pleasantries. I bring her up to speed on the Energy Triangle and my discovery the previous evening.

"If you add my whole name value together, according to my theory, the final number is seven," I explain. "Suzane's name value also comes to seven. We both know what seven plus seven total."

She waits a moment or two and continues cleaning. She asks me to describe what Sean looks like. I don't think much about it and give the best description I can.

"He was a very good-looking kid," I begin. "He had short, dark hair and dark eyes. He wore contact lenses towards the end, and kept himself in good physical shape." I also mention his multinational gene pool and his keen considerateness of others.

"He'd make a phone call on someone's birthday, and only spoke to that person; he felt the day was special to that person alone, and wouldn't talk to anyone else in the family," I recalled.

What Marilynn says next nearly floors me. "I don't know how you will take this, so I'm just going to say it."

"Say what you have to say," I encourage.

"I had a visit from Sean the other night," she admits.

"What?" I ask. To be honest, I was selfishly thinking, "Where's my visit?"

"He came to me and said: 'Hi, I'm Sean.' I know it isn't a dream or anything like that," she confides. "I sense he came to simply meet me, and for me to meet him."

I sit silently for a brief moment. "What better way to thank you for all of your help and support," I begin. "The Energy Triangle is your idea; besides, if not for you and Wanda adding bits and pieces to this story to help jog my memory, some of this stuff could've been lost in the shuffle."

"Can you bring in some pictures on Wednesday," she asks.

"They'll be on my desk for you," I reply.

After Marilynn leaves the tower, I begin to rethink what we discussed. I think about Sean's acknowledgment of Rayshal and Greg by name at the Portland seminar. I remember thinking Greg is mentioned for his help in finding the number fourteen in the formula, along with a few other tidbits of information.

I start to scribble a few notes on a sheet of paper. My interest lies in the amount of days between the Portland seminar and the two events in Seattle. These three seminars are the only time a proper name is given by Suzane during the readings.

Once again, the figures amaze me. I should know the outcome before I even start. The fact the figure matches my license plate is even more a mystery.

251 Days between Portland seminar - Northwest Afternoon T.V. program
252 Days between Portland seminar - Seattle seminar

$$251$$
$$\underline{252}$$

2+2 = **4**   5+5 = 10=1+0=**1**   1+2 = **3**
3/14 - Month & Day of Death
413 - License Plate

"Way to go, Sean!" I think aloud. "Keep those signs and validations coming – we'll make believers out of this world yet."

I ask one more favor of him. I ask if he can help me find the right publisher to get this story told.

Des Moines, Washington, Tuesday, December 2, 2003

I'm relaxing in the living room watching *"The Jerry Springer Show."* I hear a knock at the front door. I look at the clock as I make my way down the short stairway and notice it's 2:45 p.m. Wanda won't be home for another two hours.

Before I can open the door, I recognize Richard, our next-door neighbor. I haven't seen him since the church memorial for Gail Ochoa. She passed away October 8th, 2003, due to a long bout of cancer.

Richard also works for Judson Park Retirement Community. In fact, Judson Park owns the houses we both live in and pay for on a monthly basis.

It's been almost two months since the funeral. Richard and Gail had been an item for sometime. The rumor mill said they're hoping to retire together in the near future before beginning a long period of traveling around the country together.

The loss of Gail, his constant companion, closest friend and lover, has caused Richard to withdraw from the community and retreat into the privacy of his home. In order to help him cope with his grief, Judson Park has been gracious enough to allow Richard as much sick leave time as he needs.

Friends and co-workers have been unable to break through the barrier he's placed around himself. Because of the pain and grief I experienced myself over the loss of Sean, I feel I might be able to comfort him with my story in a way that nobody else can.

My hope is to help get his life's direction back on track, and to help restore some normalcy back in his life.

"Do you think it'll help if you and I go down some weekend and talk with him?" I ask Wanda. "I told him at the funeral I'm there if he needs to talk."

"That's probably a good idea," she agrees.

I guess I wasn't working fast enough for the other side; they decide to intercede and help the process along quicker.

"Richard!" I said. "How's it going?" I open the door and motion for him to come in.

Wanda had mentioned Gail's interest in the afterlife to me, and I can only assume Richard is aware of this and the two of them held similar beliefs in this area.

Our talk lasts about two hours. We talk about Gail and Sean, and how I dealt with my own grief upon losing a loved one. I also make various suggestions and ideas that might help move his own grieving process along.

"I guess you never expected to see this side of me?" I say. "Whenever we've been around one another, I've always been the jokester."

Richard agrees. "Yeah, you never come across this way."

Since Richard is a smoker, and he knows Wanda and I are not, his body language indicates it's probably a good time to draw the conversation to a close.

"By the way, did you come over here for a particular reason?" I ask, standing up from my chair. "Maybe to borrow something?"

"No," he replies. "I just had a **feeling** – I should stop by."

As soon as I close the door, I know the reason why Richard chose to come by on this day. "December second," I said aloud. "Son-of-a-gun."

$$12/02 = 12+2 = \mathbf{14}$$

Des Moines, Washington, Wednesday afternoon, December 3, 2003

I have a reference sheet of paper in hand as I proceed up Richard's front sidewalk. The door opens after my brief knock.

"I found out why you stopped by yesterday," I say.

He steps outside to join me; he follows along as I read from the notes I prepared the day before.

"Sean and Gail decided to work together to get you back on the right path," I tell him. "They combined their thought energies to break through that mind barrier you've created. That's what led you to knock on my door and listen to the message I had to give."

Richard can only smile and shake his head as the numbers I read off the paper sink in.

"I told you Gail is all around you. Only now, she's got Sean to help her out and get you back on your feet," I say.

"Maybe that's why the lights have been flashing on and off lately, as well as a few other weird things going on," he shares.

"She's just trying to get your attention to the fact that she's here with you," I respond.

$$\text{December 2, 2003} = 12/2/03 = 12+2 = \mathbf{14} \quad 03 = \mathbf{3}$$
$$\text{Gail died - } 10/08/2003 = 1+8+2+3 = \mathbf{14}$$
$$\text{Gail - } \mathbf{29} \quad \text{Ochoa - } 42 / \mathbf{24}$$
$$\text{2:45 p.m./ or 15 minutes to 3:00 p.m.} = 2+45 = 47 \quad 15\text{-}3 = 12$$
$$47+12 = 59 = 5+9 = \mathbf{14}$$

Renton tower, Thursday, December 4, 2003

I receive a thought message to check out *George Anderson's* website. He's another well known medium who also participated in the *"Afterlife Experiment"* project; I sense he might be on a seminar tour in the Pacific Northwest. "Nope," I say aloud. "Only private and group readings are scheduled."

Renton tower, Friday, December 5, 2003

I receive another thought message to check out George Anderson's website. I remembered seeing something about his latest book on

Thursday; I need something to read during my second job taking weather observations later in the day.

The drive between airports seems erratic. I'm going to a bookstore; I'm not going to a bookstore. Even though I'm running short on time, going to a bookstore wins out in the end.

I stop the car in front of the *Barnes and Noble Bookstore* in Federal Way, Washington, and I walk right to the New Age section. The books are filed alphabetically by authors' name; no such luck on this day.

"I wonder what alphabet the person stocking the shelf was using?" I think to myself.

After three complete passes, I finally do a book-to-book and shelf-to-shelf search. On the bottom shelf in the corner I find the final two copies of his book *"Lessons from the Light"* in paperback.

Sea-Tac tower, later that afternoon

I just complete this particular hour's weather observation. The cloud ceiling height is passive, meaning I won't need to take additional weather observations. I decide to see what George Anderson has to say.

The first story is about a son killed in a car accident in **1993.** "I can relate to that quite well," I think. I look at the bottom of the page; its page **19** – my story in Suzane's book began on page **19**.

I continue reading another story about a son who's also killed in a car accident; the accident takes place in the State of **Florida.** I glance down at the page number – page **24**!

The shivers ripple over my body after seeing the number representing Sean's date of birth. "Are you trying to tell me I should be taking notes while I'm reading?" I ask him aloud. "If that's the case, I'm going to the restroom first, and then I'm going downstairs to pick up a double shot of espresso at Starbucks."

After I return with coffee in hand, I jot down a few of the previous clues before I continue reading. With pencil and paper close at hand, I begin wondering what revelations await me on the next pages.

The next story is about a couple named Mary and James – they also lost a son. Mary tells her side of the story first; then James tells the story from his viewpoint. Most of the book's stories are presented this way; each story is then followed by the actual discernment (reading) by Mr. Anderson.

My mind wanders a bit after seeing the names of Mary and James together. I think of Uncle Bill, and the story he told about his grandson coming to him in a dream. The name of Uncle Bill's grandson is Mark. Mark's parents are Mary and Jim; Jim is my cousin and Uncle Bill's son.

*Mark was born 10/30/1978. He was laid to rest on 12/15/1992. He was only **14** years old. His passing is approximately **3** months before Sean will eventually cross over to the other side.*

Even though Mark was confined to a wheel chair on Earth, I'm sure he's able to jog along side of Sean in his daily fitness workout routine.

Age – **14**
Birth 10/30/78 = 1+3+7+8 = **19**
Laid to Rest 12/15/92 = 1+2+1+5+9+2 = **20**
19/20 = Pages in Suzane's Book
19+20 = **39**
39 = Sean's name/ **3** March **93** Year
Birth 10/30/1978 = 1+3+1+9+7+8 = 29
Laid to Rest 12/15/1992 = 1+2+1+5+1+9+9+2 = 30
29+30 =59 = 5+9 = **14**

It's under James' story when various **words** begin catching my eye and my thoughts. He talks about **channel surfing** on the television a few days after the funeral of his son. He comes across a medium by the name of *George Anderson.*

His story continues with a **realization of knowing** this is the medium for him; a medium who can help contact his son. He reads all of the books written by Mr. Anderson. He also tries for years to get a reading; he makes this **a mission in his life.**

After hearing about a seminar being given by Mr. Anderson, he and his wife drive **out of state** to attend. By mere coincidence, they run into Mr. Anderson on their way to a drugstore. He's **walking across the street** in front of their car.

An unsigned copy of Mr. Anderson's book lying on the front seat next to them is a good reason to roll down the window and call out his name.

I glance down at the bottom of the page – its page 59. I relate this experience with my own experience in finding a medium. I know Sean is behind it; I'm very familiar with 5 and 9 and the number they add up to.

$$5+9 = 14$$

During Mr. Anderson's discernment for Mary and James on page 65, I'm once again taken by surprise. The name **Sean** is mentioned, followed by talk about the **Celtic Language**; the word **Gaelic** is also mentioned within the paragraph.

My other interest in life is Clan Murray. Spalding is a Sept of this clan, of which I'm a participating member throughout the year. Like I told the other managers in Las Vegas, I look pretty good in a kilt!

The discernment continues with their son coming through to thank his parents for a **memorial** of some form. I immediately think of *my story tribute* to Sean and all the other people in my life who've crossed over.

A guessing game ensues between Mr. Anderson and their son on pages 68-69; he's trying to guess the child's name. His full name is *Colin O'Reilly*. I run my numbers check quickly. Colin equates to 58. O'Reilly equates to 96. It doesn't take long to receive the meaning from Sean. I'm reminded of his visit in our living room during a commercial break of *"Crossing Over with John Edward."*

$$58 \ 96 = 5+9 = 14 \quad 8+6 = 14$$
$$\text{Pages } 68\text{-}69 = 6+8+6+9 = 29$$

Glancing at the clock on the wall, I note my shift is about to end. I've got more than enough clues and information to absorb for one night.

Unable to put the book down, I read one more page. The name **Christopher** is mentioned on page 76. This is Sean's middle name. In the dictionary, Christopher refers to a patron saint of travelers – his day is July 25.

$$July\ 25 = 7/25 = 7+2+5 = \mathbf{14}$$

By this time, I already know there'll be a connection, but I put his first and middle name together on a sheet of paper, writing down the page number where each name is located in the book.

Sean – page 65   Christopher – page 76
$$6+5+7+6 = \mathbf{24}$$

Sean's Day of Birth

Chapter Fifteen
He's Still With Me

My days always begin with a prayer: I ask for the *White Light* of the *Holy Spirit, Gold Light* of *Christ Consciousness* and the *Purple Light* of *Spirituality* to surround my loved ones and I, and to protect and watch over us.

I ask the Archangel Michael to protect us all in our different forms of transportation we use daily; I ask the other Archangels to watch over us in other aspects of this life.

My prayers and thoughts go out to all the soldiers serving our country, both here and abroad. I ask that they make it home safely to their loved ones, and to give their families strength while they're away on some foreign shore in harms way.

To those who've lost loved ones, I ask God to give them the strength to continue in this life and to grant peace to their departed loved ones.

I ask that my own psychic and spiritual awareness be heightened and strengthened, so I can touch, sense and feel my family, friends and loved ones around me.

My final request is to help Sean and myself in our journey together, to tell our story, and to help everyone know that life truly goes on after death.

It's an overwhelming feeling to hear a medium speak to you with words and messages from a loved one or friend who has crossed over. The actual meaning of some clues and messages may not be known for hours, days, weeks or even months after receiving them.

Most messages are of love and reassurance. Love in the sense you carry it with you to the other side, as well as love for you to continue your own life knowing that they're still around you. Reassurance in knowing that they're well and their life is progressing.

In my case, the clues and messages from the other side sent me on a journey; a journey to contact my son to ensure he's at peace. This journey, however, turned into a lifelong mission with my son, to tell the world our story.

When a medium isn't close at hand, allowing messages to be received easily, I believe Sean tries his best to keep me focused on our objective, by sending out clues and messages in the form of numbers. These numbers represent a bright, shining star for me to follow. Nevertheless, it's still up to me to listen more intently, and to continually sharpen my awareness of things around me, while also following the thought messages I receive.

I must believe in the truth of the numbers I'm being shown. They're signs to guide me; they're showing me I'm following the right path. Sean is telling me, "I'm right beside you, Dad!"

The past week has been no exception to reassure me that Sean is behind it. There's been no medium in my life for almost three months; I can only go with what I sense and feel is actually happening.

I categorize the week into events. Richard's visit to my house is **event number #1.** My discovery of words and phrases in George Anderson's book is **event number; #2.** The order of the events can only reveal a prior knowing on the other side.

Event #1 - 12/2/2003 = 1+2+2+2+3 = 10 = 1+0 = 1
Event #2 - 12/5/2003 = 1+2+5+2+3 = 13 = 1+3 = 4

Olympia, Washington, Sunday, December 7, 2003
The day begins with memories and prayers for the military and civilian personnel who lost their lives during the Japanese sneak attack on Pearl Harbor in 1941.

My oldest step daughter Alexa is driving up from Oregon with her family to meet Wanda, her grandmother and I for lunch and a brief visit.

We decide to pick up Wanda's mother at the nursing home, where she's visiting with her husband, Wanda's step dad Joe. He's been a resident there for some time. Joe suffers from Parkinson's disease and various other age related problems. I can always get a reaction out of Joe when I walk into his room. My deep-pitched voice always gets his attention, even though his eyes are closed on most visits.

I always address him as Major Lorello, referring to his World War II military days in the European theatre. Prior to his admission to the nursing home, we spent many days discussing his various military adventures in his home and at various restaurants.

During his earlier days at the nursing home, when his health wasn't so bad, he and I would sit and harmonize post-World War II military jingles. The tune is there, although the lyrics are only vaguely remembered and one or two ad libs are necessary.

As everyone prepares to leave the room, so we're not late arriving at the restaurant, I walk out first. I wait for Wanda and her mother by the nurse's aid station at the end of the hallway.

A lady in a wheel chair stops in front of me and starts talking. "I lost my towel with my **number** on it at the dinner table," she confesses. "This other lady took my towel and gave me her towel with her **number** on it. I want my towel with my **number** on it back, so I can give her this towel with her **number** on it."

135

I can only smile at her. I mention to a nurse passing by that the lady is missing a towel. The nurse shrugs her shoulders and continues walking down the hallway; the lady in the wheel chair rolls off in a different direction.

Why would this lady use a topic like numbers or that specific word in her conversation with me? How did she know I'm the person John Holland labeled *the numbers man?*

It only takes a few seconds for me to realize what has occurred. "Thanks, Sean," I respond in my inner thoughts. "Good morning to you too, son."

$$12/7/2003 = 12+7+2+3 = \textbf{24}$$
Numbers Man
Lady in wheel chair = **1**
number + number + number + number = **4**

Renton tower, Monday, December 8, 2003
The weather is rainy and drab. It appears to be another morning in which I won't have to deal with many airplanes, and I'm just about finished reading George Anderson's book.

I open to the page which I stopped at over the weekend, a page talking about an older brother with **two sisters two years apart**. The brother's name is **Shawn**; the sister dies in **1993.**

My head shakes in disbelief. "Here we go again," I murmur. Even though the name is spelled differently, it still means the same. Sean's sisters, Rayshal and Alexa, are two years apart in age.

The following page talks about the date September 23, **1993.** The year and month are right on target; however, the birth day is one day before Sean's birth day on the 24th of September.

Pages 286-287 mention the name **Patty**. The story Anderson tells refers to the man's **fear of dying** and being taken away due to the death of his son and subsequent communications from him afterwards. There's also another reference to a **memorial** started within the last two years.

The more pages I read, the more I see **my life and references** in front of me: "A father retiring but still working"; "not particularly religious, but more spiritual than anything"; "the name Seton."

Sean's mother's maiden name was Seon. I took the "**t**" to be a reference to Sean's brother Travis.

On page 291 is a reference to something Suzane said at the Portland, Oregon seminar –"he knew his life would be short."

Page 291 = **29** & 2+1= **3**   3&9 = **93/39**
29 (Roulette) 3 (March) 93 (Year of Death) 39 (Sean alphabet number)

More validations continued with each turn of the page: "A lack of communication with your brother – he's his own worse enemy." I think about my brother Gary – the reference couldn't be more correct; "most **profound signs** come when you least expect"; "you like working with bereaved parents"; "working through your grief **independently** rather than working along with a support group" – **I see you writing!**

There's a reference to **stuffed animals.** My family room is loaded with these furry creatures, especially my favorite *Steiff collection.* These toy animals are made in Germany, and each animal is marked with a special *yellow Steiff tag* in the ear.

The final clues are enough to quiet my critics as far as I'm concerned; the name **Josh** is referenced on one of the pages. Sean's step brother, through Pat and Rob, is named Josh.

Toward the end of this final discernment by Mr. Anderson, the topic involves **the communication to the mother."** At the *Northwest Afternoon seminar,* Sean thanks me for my efforts in communicating with his mother to keep her abreast of what's happening.

―――――――

I stop by the post office on my way home to mail a letter to the **publishers** of Suzane Northrop's book. This letter offers background about my story, along with a few teasers to capture their attention, in the hope of creating an interest in the idea of Suzane's next book: **a compilation of short stories**, submitted by her followers, with Suzane as co-author editing the stories in her own unique style of writing.

My intent is to create a strong enough interest to help persuade Suzane to make the decision to become a co-author in this venture. I assure the publisher's president that Suzane and her assistant Linda are aware of my intent to have this story told in such a narrative.

The date of the letter makes me feel very confidant as I drop it in the mail slot.

$$12/8/03 = 1+2+8 +3 = \mathbf{14}$$

Des Moines, Washington, Monday, later that afternoon.

It's still early afternoon when I pull in the driveway. The mailman is just pulling away from the mailbox and I retrieve the mail before walking inside.

Wanda won't be home for a few more hours. Our plans are to watch the first ever *John Edward pay-per-view special* this evening. Suzane Northrop is making a special guest appearance at the end; I plan to tape the event and take it down to my neighbor Richard the next day.

Glancing down at the stack of mail in front of me, one card in particular stands out; it's from my sister Diane's son Tim. It's a wedding invitation for the summer of 2004. I chuckle to myself when I read the date.

"Hello," says the voice on the phone.

"It's me, your brother out west!" I said in my usual sarcastic voice. "I just called to tell you I received your son's wedding invitation."

"You and Wanda are going, right?" she asks.

"As of now we are," I reply. "In fact, the reason I called is to let you know the wedding date adds up to fourteen. If I'm there, it's got to be a good omen for Tim."

My sister utters her normal, "Good, God!" I'm still trying to figure out if she means it good naturedly, or condescendingly.

Before disconnecting, she provides a little tidbit of her own. "I'm quitting my job for a new position with another company," she reveals. "Matter of fact, my last day at work is December 15th. There's **another fourteen** for your story!"

I took *that comment* in a condescending way.

$$\text{The days date - } 12/8/03 = 1+2+8+3 = \mathbf{14}$$
$$\text{The wedding date - } 7/10/2004 = 7+1+2+4 = \mathbf{14}$$
$$\text{Final work day } – 12/15/2003 = 1+2+1+5+2+3 = \mathbf{14}$$
$$\text{3 dates of } \mathbf{14} = 14+14+14 = 42$$
$$\text{42 reversed } = \mathbf{24} \text{ (Sean's birth date)}$$

Des Moines, Washington, Tuesday, December 9, 2003

After arriving home from work, I decide to take the John Edward tape up to Richard. I hope it will help raise his spirits, as well as give him a little insight on Suzane Northrop.

We spend about a half hour talking in his living room. He informs me he'll be going back to work in late December after Christmas.

"My suggestion would be to take a few baby steps in the interim," I said. "Visit a few friends and co-workers next door for a couple of minutes each day. This will get you back in the flow, and prepare you for the attention and questions that will come."

Upon returning home I check for email. I'm always looking for something from Suzane's assistant Linda.

"Nothing," I comment to myself. "Oh, well."

I'm about to log off the computer when a familiar feeling passes over me. I pull up a website I rarely visit, **www.angeltherapy.com**. This is Doreen Virtue's site, another renowned psychic.

I notice on her schedule of upcoming events that Sean is already making plans for something to happen in November 2004.

An event entitled *"Mystical Connection,"* is planned. This will involve a full day of psychic readings by Doreen Virtue, Gordon Smith from Great Britain, Sonia Choquette and another favorite of mine, John Holland.

The event is scheduled to take place November 14th from 9:00 a.m. until 5:30 p.m. Ticket prices will vary from $25 to $75 per person.

I mark the event on my calendar to insure I don't forget to pre-order the tickets. Wanda and I will be ordering the $75 tickets; I've learned to follow Sean's lead without question.

November **14**

11/14/04 = **ones** and **fours**

9-5:30 = 9+5 = **14**   30 = 3+0 = **3**

$75.00 + $75.00 = 7+7 = **14**   5+5 = 10 = 1+0 = **1** (ones and fours)

$75.00 + $75.00 = 7+5+7+5 = **24**

Chapter Sixteen
From a Short Story to a Book

The year 2004 arrives very quickly. I look back over 2003 at the discoveries, hardships and loss it brought into my life, and I thank God how truly blessed I am today. Nevertheless, I still have many crossroads and roadblocks ahead.

I'm still trying to work things out with Suzane. I feel the revelation at the seminar in Seattle involving Sean showing a book should've been the catalyst to make her realize a book venture between the two of us could be a very good thing.

Sadly to say, she doesn't have the whole picture; she's only aware of certain parts of my story. My family and I are the only ones aware of the overwhelming clues pointing in one direction and pointing to one source.

Des Moines, Washington, Monday, January 5, 2004
Wanda's been in Olympia the past five weeks because her step-father Joe has taken a turn for the worse. Her mother refuses to

leave his bedside until the end, and Wanda feels an obligation to do the same for her mother and Joe as well.

Rayshal calls at 8:30 p.m. choking back tears. "He's gone," she sobs.

"What time?" I ask.

"About fifteen minutes ago," she says.

Joseph James Lorello leaves this world at 8:15 p.m. The signs tell me that Sean is there to greet him at the crossover point into the next life.

$$8:15 \text{ p.m.} = 8+1+5 = \mathbf{14}$$

Des Moines, Washington, Thursday night, January 8, 2004

I sit at the computer to enter Joe's name into my ongoing story line, but first I say a silent prayer in his memory.

Before logging off, I ask Sean to help with a response from Suzane regarding a request I made through her assistant Linda. It's been almost two weeks since I emailed my question.

My AOL mailbox appears a few minutes later, and there's an email from Linda! I mentally thank Sean for his help.

As I log off the computer for the night, I ask Sean to keep sending clues. "It helps to keep my focus on our objective, son."

Before drifting off to sleep in our upstairs bedroom, I channel surf the TV and find the Kevin Costner movie *"Field of Dreams."* There's an hour and fifteen minutes left to watch. I always enjoy the movie, especially the end – a line of cars with their headlights illuminated, snaking out for miles on the road leading to the farm.

This would always bring back memories of our yearly Halloween event in Klamath Falls. Visitors would mention how the adjoining streets are lined with cars trying to get to our house.

As the movie progresses, I begin to see subtle clues from Sean. "I need to take you there," says Costner's character Ray to Terrance Mann, played by James Earl Jones, "but it's a **good story!**" At the ballpark, another **message** is given to Ray via the scoreboard **sign**.

I've seen the movie many times, but I never had the awareness to listen for any clues (or signs) being given. Ray and Terry are in the van returning to Iowa. Ray talks about his argument with his father: "I was **fourteen** at the time."

Finally, as Terrance Mann walks off into the cornfield, Ray tells him he wants a **complete written story** on what he finds in the afterlife.

$$1/8/2004 = 1+8 = 9 \quad 2004 = 24$$
$$1+2 = 3 \quad 1\&4 = 14 \quad 1+8 = 9 \quad 1+2 = 3$$
$$\mathbf{9/24 \ \& \ 3/14/93}$$

Renton tower, Friday, January 16, 2004

After checking the Renton tower email I check my personal account. In my AOL account is a letter from Jodere Publishing group; my hopes are high as I press the read box.

They like the idea of our story but write, "While it is a delightful concept, it is not along the lines of the books we are looking to publish at this time."

My horoscope for the day reads: "It's an excellent time for setting goals even though you may feel like you're **benched.**"

$$\text{January 16, 2004} = 1/16/2004 = 1+1+6+2+4 = \mathbf{14}$$

Des Moines, Washington, Sunday, January 18, 2004

Before Wanda and I leave the house for the day, I reply to Linda's earlier email and relay the bad news. I ask Linda if Suzane is aware of Jodere's decision. Three hours later I read, "Yes, she's aware of their decision."

Later that night, before going to bed I glance at the day's horoscope. "You have just a few more days of relative obscurity before you emerge into the spotlight. Use them well."

One week later

I begin reviewing the submission prerequisites for certain publishers and learn that to meet their various requirements, I'll have to divide my two-part story into chapters.

"A few more days of obscurity," I think to myself. "If that's Sean's way of giving me a message, how long is a "few days" in our conception of time as compared to his?

The rewrite of each chapter begins taking form, and as I remember various omitted items, I fill in the gaps with this new information. My short story is slowly turning into a complete book. I begin to realize the true meaning of the seminar revelation: **the book** Sean reveals to Suzane isn't a collection of short stories by her followers, but it's our **own story in book form.**

"Was it a proposed book he showed?" I wonder. "Or was it a published edition?" My thoughts refer back to the rest of the horoscope – "before you emerge into the spotlight."

If I'm to believe the horoscope to be true, I must accept the rejection by the Jodere Group publisher. I must also believe Sean needed to get my attention. The handwriting has been on the wall all the time; I just misinterpreted the meaning. He knew I didn't have our story prepared in the right format, and our story was getting too long for publication as a short story.

Des Moines, Washington, Saturday morning, February 7, 2004
Walking into the kitchen, I notice Wanda reading the morning newspaper. Pouring myself a cup of coffee, I stand behind her for a moment before asking, "Would you like to hear about the dream I just had?"

Taking off her reading glasses, she sets them on the counter, takes another sip of coffee and gives me her undivided attention.

"I'm back in Samoa. The tower is much larger. There are televisions and video monitors all over the place. The 2nd floor area seems to be under construction.

I'm downstairs changing clothes and talking with another person. I feel like I'm going to be late relieving the controller upstairs. Because I want to be on time at 35 minutes after the hour, I head upstairs half dressed with my shirt open.

Partway up, I stop to put on my shoes – they're black. Suddenly, I'm in a garage. A helium filled ball is trying to fly out of the door, and there are many items around me I can't describe.

When I get to the tower cab, there are lots of people standing around. I can see the Island of Samoa through the tower window; the runway seems to be farther away from the tower and surrounded by a low cloud of fog.

The controller on duty is talking with an aircraft flying in from Western Samoa, a neighboring island. He's also talking with a passenger-bound aircraft inbound from Hawaii, about one hundred miles north of the island.

I can see both aircraft simultaneously. It appears I'm peering out from the Western Samoa aircraft. Within a few seconds, I'm looking out the tower windows at the newly constructed, modern looking shacks alongside the airport property. I also see new buildings across the other side of the airport.

"What are all of these buildings and shacks?" I ask.

"They're new stores and office buildings," one of the people reply.

"Wanda's sure going to like this," I say.

As I walk past the controller on duty communicating with the airplanes, I notice the old television set dating from my previous tour of duty during the eighties. It's broken, and there's a new television sitting on top of it. I noticed the size of the TV, the dials and a program airing at the time.

My eyes glance into the next room. "This is new," I think to myself. "It wasn't there in the eighties." I see long tables surrounded by chairs and lots of tall lockers. I remember thinking, "This is where they must eat their meals."

A large Samoan takes a group of us to a large communication panel in the room. He's showing everyone how to set a **WWV Clock.** *He demonstrates which buttons need to be pushed and when. The WWV are call letters for a radio station at Ft. Collins, Colorado. They broadcast the universal time clock continuously.*

I remember thinking, to myself how easy it'll be to figure out. As he starts to walk away, he says: "There's **29** *days in February this year. Make sure you set the clock appropriately." I remember* *looking at his profile as he passes. His cheeks were dark, as was his hair.*

I'm in another room where two ladies are working side by side. One lady is working a radar scope and separating airplanes. The other lady is watching a screen that looks like a television; however, it's some form of a radar-tracking unit with real time tracking.

*"Do you feel your duty is **to help people** here on the island?" asks one of the lady controllers looking in my direction.*

"I feel like an ambassador," I respond. "I'll deal with the people and keep that kind of feeling in mind."

The lady seated in front of the strange television looking unit agrees with my response. Within a second or two, something takes place on her screen; she ceases her conversation with me and gives her full attention to the on-screen situation.

In the blink of an eye, I'm outside looking at two very small experimental jets taxiing out to the runway. I'm not on the ground; I feel as if I'm airborne. I look inside the small cockpit window. I'm talking with the pilot, whose back is to me. I see a very sophisticated instrument panel, along with a television screen that seems to show everything viewable to the front of the aircraft. The pilot appears to be well-educated, an engineer knowledgeable type.

I watch him walk to the back of the plane for coffee. The interior of the plane seems like the length of two football fields, while the aircraft's exterior appears to be the size of a small, single engine Cessna.

*While he's standing at the back of the aircraft, I ask about the bathroom facilities. I also notice we're airborne surrounded by clouds. I'm still on the outside of the aircraft. **End of Dream***

Conclusion: *I feel Sean is showing me how our story process is working. Even though he's on the outside, he's still able to look in and know what's taking place.*

The cockpit seemed empty for a short time, but the airplane is still heading in the right direction. I may not sense Sean's presence all the time, but, my faith in knowing he's with me keeps my focus and awareness going forward.

Clues: *The dream occurred Friday night/Saturday morning:*

Friday - 2/6/2004 = 2+6+2+4 = **14**
Saturday – 2/7/2004 = 2+7+2+4 = 15
14 + 15 = **29**
Clock date reference - February **29** *days*
35 minute shift reference – Sean's age today **35**
WWV (Clock) = W = 23   V = 22 = 23+23+22 = 68 = 6+8 = **14**

I don't know what tomorrow is going to bring regarding our book or when it will be completed. I only know our story doesn't stop here. I'll continue to maintain a total awareness of my inner thoughts and outer surroundings for clues and messages each day of my life.

Sean is definitely a part of my life. We've got a story worth telling and a story worth believing. Now more than ever I need to get this short story converted to book form so we can have a story worth reading.

"If our story will bring comfort to only one person in my lifetime," I think, "then all the writes and rewrites I have to do will be worth it."

147

Chapter Seventeen
Memories and Signs

I glance at the alarm clock on the nightstand: 4:59 a.m. I'm still amazed how my body clock at 58 years old still functions properly, especially after working two jobs over the past ten months – and that's not including all the overtime I've put in with both jobs to cover personnel shortages.

Wanda is lying next to me. I reach up to turn the alarm switch off so it won't wake her a minute later. Before my feet hit the floor, I say my morning prayer. These morning and night prayers have helped me deal with the gut wrenching emotional issues I've wrestled with since losing Sean in 1993.

$$4:59 \text{ a.m.}$$
$$4= 4 \quad 59= 5+9= \mathbf{14}$$
$$4 \ \& \ 14 = 2 \ (4\text{'s}) = \mathbf{24}$$

The East Coast - West Coast distance between Sean and I when he was alive never was an issue; we were always in contact with each other. Even after the government moved the rest of my family to Pago Pago, American Samoa, our communication never stopped.

Because of this constant communication when he was part of this world, why should it stop between us simply because our worlds have changed?

After prayers I perform my normal morning routine, or so I think. I slowly drag my body down the hallway toward the kitchen. The coffee has to be brewing before Wanda gets out of bed or she won't be able to function.

For some reason, I sense this day might be a little different than most. Why? I really don't have a clue. I only have a complete trust in my senses and awareness of things happening around me; a trust I've come to rely on heavily after being led to Sean in Portland in 2003.

Walking to my favorite living room chair, I contentedly take a seat and stare out the front window, enjoying a few minutes of complete silence.

Once again I gaze out on the waters making up parts of the Puget Sound, along with occasional white cumulus clouds rustling by in the distance. This scene always seems to relax me and allow my problems to melt away, if only for a moment. Before long I'm lost in my thoughts…

It's been almost one year to the day when I found myself seated in this same chair at 2 a.m., driven by an unseen force I couldn't explain, trying to sort out the number clues Sean was leaving me. Rayshal and I had attended a seminar by Suzane two days earlier on Monday. I took her there because Wanda was out of town with her mother for medical reasons. It gave me a chance to introduce Rayshal to my world of mediums and how they operate, as well as try to prepare her to possibly continue along the same lines after my own passing.

On our drive to Seattle, I said a silent prayer to Sean to come through for his sister, since I already had a partial reading over the telephone in 2002, thanks to a local radio station who invited Suzane to be a guest on their local talk show.

The Monday seminar proved to be uneventful for us; nevertheless, Rayshal and I both enjoyed what we witnessed; as a side note, her belief in the next world seemed to elevate a little higher in her thought process.

It wasn't until the next day at the tower that I realized my choice of the word "uneventful" describing the seminar was wrong. On pages 19 and 20 of her latest book, Suzane had written two examples of communication from the other side in the form of numbers.

These examples were my own experiences; experiences I shared on a web site with people who believe as I do. I just wanted to have some feedback on the possibility that Sean was communicating to me through numbers.

*Because I couldn't sleep on this particular night, I wandered out to the living room and sat down in hopes of clearing my thoughts. After a few minutes, it finally hits me – a blast of white light ignites my inner brain, and **numbers** begin to cascade through my thoughts like a waterfall.*

The message becomes clear. I'd take the short trip to Portland on Friday after work to attend Suzane's seminar. This gathering would be her final seminar in the Pacific Northwest before joining John Edward, as well as two other top mediums from across the country, in a day long seminar extravaganza in Las Vegas.

Wanda walks out of the bedroom to see what's wrong. "I think I'm supposed to go to the seminar in Portland on Friday?" I tell her.

"Why?" she responds with a yawn.

*"The numbers make me feel something special might happen. It's like their telling me, **I've got to be there**; besides, I can pick up a few more copies of her book for Pat and my brother since he helped find my missing number," I reply.*

"If you feel that strongly about it, I think you should go on down," Wanda agrees.

"Besides everything else, Friday is two weeks before the tenth anniversary of his death," I remind her. *"Meaning?"* asks Wanda. *"Two weeks is **fourteen**...there's the number **14** again!"*

*Two weeks is **fourteen***

Even though the above journey into the afterlife ends with a successful contact with Sean, I continue to enjoy his presence around me. He's continually providing me with clues and information, almost on a daily basis it seems; in my opinion, that proves life exists after death.

Unlike my previous adventure, where I was searching for my own interests, our new path together will be to help others **in his world** get their messages out to their own loved ones **in my world** – messages about love, hope, and being around and waiting to be discovered in a relationship such as ours.

In addition, the **messages** sent by Sean through the use of our number theory will continue to be documented and shared with the world in book form. These messages, or "simple hello's through numbers," will be **his signature;** my proof that the occurrence, or message, comes from his place of residence.

"Good idea," I think aloud. "Great title for book number two: *MESSAGES FROM THE NEXT WORLD His Signature."*

Renton tower, Friday morning, February 20th, 2004
I just finish making the opening announcement that'll begin another day of controlling airplanes. It's raining outside, so I'm preparing for an easy workday. Friday is my short workday of the week; I only have to put in four hours today.

As I glance out the large tower windows and watch the threatening, dark cumulus clouds pass, a thought crosses my mind: I envision the seminar in June with John Holland; I also think about the **all day seminar** that's also coming in November. I write myself another reminder to purchase the event tickets early.

"My family and friends can surely get a message through during these events," I think aloud, "especially given the November seminar is nine-and-a-half hours long."

The November seminar has four famous mediums performing that day. One in particular comes to mind: *Gordon Smith, "The Psychic Barber."*

I recall an article I read last year in November from the publisher's web site promoting the event. It said that Gordon Smith was from Glasgow, Scotland, and was considered a very promising up and coming medium. His trade name *The Psychic Barber* was derived from him owning a barbershop in downtown Glasgow.

"Let's see if he's got a web site," I think, as my fingers type **www.gordonsmith.com** on the keyboard and watch it display in the URL address field on the screen. His web site appears a few moments later. Opening a tab promoting his book, *"Psychic Barber Spirit Messenger,"* I began reading the various captions, including one slugged, *"7th son of 7th son"*.

This message couldn't be any clearer. I'll need to stop by the *Barnes & Noble* bookstore in Federal Way before I go to my weather job later this afternoon. This book should help me get acquainted with the man before his appearance in Seattle later this year. I believe anything I can do to make it easier for my son, family or friends to contact me, I'll do.

$$7^{th} \text{ son of } 7^{th} \text{ son} = 7 + 7 = \mathbf{14}$$

Des Moines, Washington, Sunday, March 14, 2004
Today marks the eleventh anniversary of Sean's death. I ordered the flowers for his grave site from Carlene's Florist in Warrior, Alabama on Friday. I really enjoy my short conversations with Carlene. I owe her the world for taking care of Sean these past eleven years. I told her when our book comes out she'll be famous.

"I'll make you a star so everyone across the country will know about your flower shop," I tease. "I'll also make sure I send you a special autographed copy of the book so you can display it in your shop."

I've been working overtime in hopes of getting out from under the burden of debt we've gotten ourselves into. The extra money seems to be making a major dent in our overall obligations; nevertheless, it comes with a price.

Being a typical weekend, with me working both Saturday and Sunday, Wanda is in Olympia visiting her mother. I told her she didn't have to stay around the house all weekend waiting for me to come home.

"Why don't you pack your bags on Friday and drive to your mothers for the weekend," is my usual Thursday night encouragement.

She works harder than I do at her job at Judson Park. She needs to unwind during her days off, and staying at home adjacent to her place of employment viewable from our front window isn't going to do it on the weekends.

Between the two of us, we try to get the household chores done during the week so our weekends are free from these mundane activities.

I give Wanda an early courtesy call to let her know Travis is stopping by this afternoon with Kaila, Wanda's youngest and closest granddaughter. She'll be turning three later this year in mid-June.

Even though the house will get a little crazy later in the day, when **Poppa** and **Gamma** get her running around and screaming, we'll all have our own personal thoughts regarding Sean's passing in the back of our mind, and how we all miss his **physical presence** here on Earth.

3/14/93

Chapter Eighteen

Good-bye to my Mother; Hello from Another

Des Moines, Washington, Monday, March 15, 2004

It's early in the afternoon when I walk through the front door and notice the message light on the phone blinking. My sister Diane has left us a tearful message that our mom has just taken a turn for the worse at the nursing home where she resides.

The phone rings before I can call Diane back. Its Diane's husband Bob; the time is 2:00 p.m.

"It's not looking good, Denny," Bob tells me. "The doctors give her twenty-four to forty-eight hours. If you want to see her alive you better start making arrangements."

We talked a few more minutes to discuss some minor details, and then I put an emergency call through to Wanda's work to let her know the situation.

Within the hour, we had reservations on United Air Lines to fly out of Seattle at 11 p.m. that night. We'd arrive in Cleveland around 9 a.m. Tuesday, March 16th.

Our three places of employment were appraised of the situation and immediately approved bereavement leave for us both. When Wanda arrives home at 5 p.m., I'm already packed. I'm standing in the kitchen making sure I've got all of our medication for the trip when the phone rings at 5:30 p.m.; it's Bob calling again from Cleveland.

"She's gone, Denny, I'm sorry," he relates. "Can you let Greg know?"

"Yeah, I'll call him and let him know," I agreed.

Nothing more needed to be said; I hang up the phone and say a silent prayer for my Mom. I walk slowly towards the back bedroom to let Wanda know that Mom has died. While Wanda continues to pack I make the necessary phone calls to Greg, Travis, Rayshal and Alexa.

Greg is driving to Ohio from Chicago. His family will follow a day or so later after the funeral arrangements have been made. Greg is the same brother that helped decipher the missing number 14 in my theory when it all began to unravel in June, 2002.

"Greg, where are you now?" I ask.

"I just got on the turnpike a minute or so ago," he replies.

"Why don't you pull off to the side for a moment?"

"Oh, shit!" he responds despondently. "She's gone?"

"Yes, a few minutes ago," I said.

"I might as well turn around and go back and get the family now," he says before disconnecting without a good-bye.

I can understand his anguish. I'm hoping he'll be okay for the one-hour drive back to his home in Streator.

$$3/20/1920 - \text{Mom's date of birth}$$
$$3/15/2004 - \text{Mom's date of death}$$
$$3+2+0+1+9+20 = 17 = 1+7 = 8 \quad 3+1+5+2+0+0+4 = 15 = 1+5 = 6$$
$$8+6 = \textbf{14} - \text{Sean's day of Death}$$
$$3/15/2004 = 3+1+5 = \textbf{9} \quad 2004 = \textbf{24}$$
$$9/24 = \text{September 24} - \text{Sean's Birthday}$$

My sister Bonnie picks us up at the airport in Cleveland the following morning. Snow began falling the previous night, and snowflakes the size of pancakes drop silently as we file to the parking garage, bags in tow. I'm able to completely reassure myself about my move to the Pacific Northwest twenty-seven years earlier.

"I sure made the right choice in 1977," I think to myself.

$$77 = 7+7 = \mathbf{14}$$
$$1977 = 1+9+7+7 = \mathbf{24}$$

The funeral services are tentatively scheduled for Friday morning. Because Diane lives in the same community as the nursing home, all roads lead to Mentor, Ohio. For the next several days, Diane's house is the new KOA campground; the meeting place for all our siblings and their families.

Mentor, Ohio, Thursday, March 18, 2004
Most of our family and relatives are gathered around the dining room table late in the afternoon exchanging stories and sharing a few drinks to pass the time.

The minister conducting the services for my mother on Friday is scheduled to stop by for a review of last minute funeral arrangements, and to gather input our family might have regarding a eulogy.

I'd promised my Aunt Alby that Wanda and I will stop to pay our respects before we see her at the funeral on Friday; she lives a few houses down the street from my sister.

The minister is running a little late, so I place a phone call to Aunt Alby to reassure her we're still planning on stopping to visit. "We're running a little bit behind schedule," I tell her, "but the minister just got here so it won't be too much longer."

"Thanks for calling, Denny," she replies. "I was beginning to wonder if you were going to show up."

The last time Wanda and I saw Aunt Alby and Uncle Bill was at my older brother Jack's funeral in May, 2002. He died of a massive heart attack at a wedding reception for our nephew Bobby, my sister's oldest son.

I wrote Jack's eulogy a few days before leaving Seattle. I knew the normal religious ceremonial offerings wouldn't do him justice, especially the way he lived his life with a cup of coffee in one hand and a cigarette in the other.

This needed to be a tribute from the next brother in line; a tribute the entire family and friends would remember for some time. And remember they did!

"I just called Aunt Alby and told her we're running a little late," I advised Wanda. "She's only about fifteen houses down the road."

Diane and Bob own the house on Clearair Drive originally built by our parents in the late fifties. Due to family problems and personal circumstances following our father's death, my sister arranged to prevent foreclosure of the property and the relinquishing of any financial obligations on our mother, who planned to live there until her own passing or health problems preventing her from taking care of herself.

My dad chose to have their house built in the same neighborhood as his brother. It also provided an opportunity for my siblings and me to attend the same high school from which Dad graduated.

My thought is interrupted when the lady minister walks in and stands momentarily in the dining room before taking a seat; my sister introduces everyone seated at the table.

When the minister's gaze falls on me, I can **sense** a momentary pause, as if the wheels in her brain spin to catch up, ultimately helping her to remember.

"Can I ask you a favor?" I ask the minister sincerely.

"I'm listening," she responds hesitantly, as if her brain waves are flashing a bright red warning inside her head.

"Is it okay if **I don't stand up** at the service tomorrow, and **I don't say anything**?" I work to keep my tone serious, having arranged this little put-on with my siblings a few minutes earlier.

The minister appeared uncomfortable around our kidding and joking, but she did share a funny tidbit of her own regarding our brother Jack's funeral.

*A few days after Jack's funeral, she's called into a meeting with the funeral director and staff. They decide that any future requests by family members **of any family** wishing to speak about their loved ones will be offered a maximum of five minutes.*

*This new policy is called **The Dennis Policy**, named for yours truly. I can envision Jack having a few laughs on the other side after hearing this news.*

Uncle Bill Remembered - The Dennis Policy in force

Brunner Funeral Home, Mentor, Ohio, Friday afternoon, March 19, 2004

I'm amazed at the family, friends and relatives that have taken time from their busy schedules to come and pay their respects to my mother.

I sense Sean is also here to let me know Mom is in safe hands and isn't alone. I find it easy to talk with friends and relatives I haven't seen in years about my spirituality issue, as well as my new book in the making.

When my cousin Jim, Uncle Bill's son, stops to offer his condolences, I offer my own in regards to his father.

"I really wanted to make it back for his funeral," I said. "Especially because he liked the way I give a eulogy."

I also mention to Jim the tribute I offer in my book for his son Mark and his Dad.

"Oh wow, that sounds great," Jim replies. "Can I go get Mary so you can tell her about this?"

"Sure, go ahead."

Ever since Jim and Mary lost their son Mark in December, 1992 at the age of **fourteen**, Mary has continually struggled with the issue. Mark was confined to a wheelchair most of his life. Because of logistics and geography, I never got to see him.

Jim's hoping my revelation will help his wife cope with their loss. Mark was taken from her **three months** before Sean was taken from me.

From the number connections I've established, though, I know for a fact that Sean and Mark are jogging alongside each other on their daily fitness workout routine in the Next World.

Three months / **fourteen**

I ask Mary to join me at the back of the hall where we can have a little privacy.

I tell her a short version of my story and my journey to find Sean. I then bring up my book, specifically the references regarding Uncle Bill and Mark.

"I feel it's important," I confess. "It's a tribute to my son, as well as your son and everyone else I reference or talk about during this journey."

I can see tears beginning to form in Mary and Jim's eyes as I'm sharing this. "When I get back to Washington, I'll send you, Jim and Aunt Alby excerpts from the book mentioning Mark and Uncle Bill," I offer.

Their forced smiles through the tears said it all. I didn't have to ask for their approval to use Mark's name. A sincere hug from the two of them sealed their acceptance and a closer bond between us.

It's time to start the service. The siblings sit in the front row according to age. I'm on the outside, followed by the twins and our two sisters. Our immediate family members found places somewhere behind this first row of chairs.

A chair to my right was left vacant for Jack. Wanda sent a message through my nephew for me to get a **single rose** from one of the bouquets at the front of the room to place on this seat to honor Jack.

"Don't let me pull this whole display over in front of everyone," I prayed silently. Luckily, the spirit world was with me and the single rose came right out of the fixed bouquet.

At the minister's mention of his name during her eulogy, I raise the rose heavenward for all to see, and to offer a few short seconds to his memory and presence in the room. This gesture brings tears to the eyes to all who knew Jack, especially his son and daughters seated behind me with memories of their father's casket along the adjoining wall to their right.

My own tears flow as I listen to the minister's words about Mother's life, hopes and dreams; through teary eyes I scan the many pictures memorializing her almost eighty-five years here on Earth.

Rest in peace, Mom!

After the minister speaks her final words, she invites guests to attend a meal and reception with the family in the upstairs meeting room. I'm seated at the table with my brother Greg when I catch sight of a lady whose name I couldn't remember.

"That's Rita," Greg says. "She's Mike's wife."

"Mike?" I question.

"Becky's brother." Greg continues. "He died several years before Becky died."

Having been away from Mentor for so long, my memories of family, friends and relatives have become hazy and ragged.

Becky was married to my brother Jack. She passed away about a year before my brother. Rita would be the aunt to my nephew and niece, John David and Rebecca, who are Becky and Jack's children; both are now over twenty-one.

Even though Mike's death took place many years ago, Rita is still having a problem coping with his loss. I can empathize with her situation without casting stones.

"Thanks for coming Rita," I said while reaching out to shake her hand.

"Denny, I wouldn't miss it," she responds. "Your mom meant the world to me."

She led me by the hand to introduce her daughter and her daughter's finance'. After a little small talk, the daughter mentioned her upcoming marriage the beginning of next month.

I smiled and gave her a congratulatory hug. While hugging her, I see the church alter in my mind with a picture of her father Mike on an easel to be seen by the bride as she walks down the aisle.

By now, Rita is tugging on my coattail excitedly moving in an up and down motion. "Guess who gets to walk her down the aisle?" she asks breathlessly.

I smile at her while this **image** is still fresh in my mind. "Are you going to have a picture of Mike at the altar to see his little girl walking down the aisle?" I ask innocently.

"Are you out of your mind?" she quickly replies. "Do you want me to lose it right there in the church in front of everybody?"

Before I had a chance to open my mouth and explain, Rita's daughter comes to my defense. "I've been thinking the same thing, Mom," she admits.

"Thinking what?" Rita asks, her eyebrows slowly rising as her head turns slightly to one side.

"What he just said...about the picture of Dad being on the altar."

Tears form in Rita's eyes. "I didn't know you've been thinking about that?" she admits.

"I didn't know how to tell you; especially with the emotional issue with Dad and you," she says.

I take Rita aside for a moment and give her a brief update on the current happenings in my life. "The Spirit World works in funny ways," I relate. "Maybe Mike felt this to be the right opportunity to get his message to you before it's too late."

Rita tells me a story that happened at Mike's bedside during his final hours of life. "I'm going to be at my daughter's wedding...**I promise**," he said, knowing it would be many years in the future since his daughter was only eleven at the time.

"I guess he used me to help open the door to the idea," I reply.

Rita hugs me for making her aware of her daughter's thoughts and wishes. "I'll be giving this a lot of thought over the next few weeks," she confides.

Wanda and I ride with Diane and Bob back to their house for another family gathering, but this one with less people. I relate the story about my talk with Rita to the three of them. Bob, as usual, could only laugh about this whole spirit thing going on in my life.

"Laugh all you want," I warn. "One of these days your Mom is going to come through and tell me what you whispered in her ear at her bedside – then you're going to change your thinking!"

"I truly doubt that," he laughs sarcastically.

Later in the evening at Bob and Diane's house, I mention my talk with Rita to John David.

"Yeah, Aunt Rita already told me about it," he says. "I just told her my Uncle Denny has this uncanny way of knowing the right thing to say at various times."

He also told me he'll be attending Rita's daughter's wedding, and he'll keep me informed about the picture and the altar happenings.

Thanks to Mom and Sean, I felt very good regarding the work I accomplished on a very sad day in my life.

3/18/2004 – Mom's cremation
3 = March
18 = 1+8 = **9** = September
2004 = **24**
3/**19**/2004 – Mom's funeral service
3/**20**/2004 – Mom's birthday (died 5 days prior to 84th birthday)
19/20 – Pages in Suzane's book
19+20 = **39** = Sean's name/ 3-March/ 93-year

Chapter Nineteen
The Blue Butterfly

We stayed in Ohio a few extra days after the funeral. After returning to the Pacific Northwest, as promised I put together an excerpt from my story involving Mark Spalding (my Cousin Jim's son), and sent it to Jim and Mary.

I mailed it on Wednesday, March 24, 2004. I decided to call Aunt Alby and read to her the portion about Uncle Bill since her vision seemed to be getting worse.

"You have a beautiful way of expressing yourself," she compliments after the reading.

March 24, 2004 = 3/**24**/2004
3/24 = 3+2+4= **9**   2004 = 2+0+0+2 = **24**
9/24 = Sean's month & day of birth

Des Moines, Washington, Friday, March 26, 2004

After leaving the control tower at Renton airport, I decide to make a quick stop at the Starbucks located at the top of the hill leading to my house before heading home.

As I pull into the parking lot, I observe two college-age women sitting at one of the outside tables adjacent to the entrance. As I approach, I notice the midriff of the girl facing away from me reveals *a large, blue Butterfly tattoo.*

As you may recall, during the month of February 2003, I attended a seminar in Seattle conducted by Suzane Northrop. Wanda was out of town with her mother, so I asked Rayshal if she'd like to accompany me to the seminar.

*While nothing eventful happened for either of us, we both purchased a copy of her latest book; I took my copy to work the next day. On page eighteen, the topic pertained to **numbers** being used as a form of contact with and from the Spirit World.*

Since my life is overpowered with number clues at the moment, I quickly recalled my own list of number communications and sat up with greater interest.

On page nineteen is a reference to the contact I had with my son. I didn't have to read the whole page to know the story was about me – without using my name. I turned the page and noted that our visit from Sean via the television set is also included.

*After leaving work early, I knew I had to contact Pat, Sean's birth mother, to let her know her son is referenced in a published book by a well-known author. Before we said our good-byes, Pat shared a story about **a blue butterfly;** each time she visits Sean's grave site a blue butterfly flutters nearby.*

A smile lights my face as I walk through the door; I say good afternoon to Sean in my thoughts as I approach the counter. I order my usual two-shot, grande Americano with light room; I walk to the self-service counter and add the half inch of fat-free milk and three

Equals® before retracing my steps to the parking lot. The butterfly tattooed woman and her friend are gone.

Upon arriving home I jot down my experience with the blue butterfly in my log; I also look up the date when Sean's mom first mentioned the story about the butterfly.

Transfixed on the date, I can sense Sean's spirit around me as the meaning etches itself in my mind. It's taken **thirteen months** for the Blue Butterfly to find its way to the Pacific Northwest. I relate my discovery to Wanda a few hours later when she returns home after work.

February **26,** 2003 – Pat's story
March **26,** 2004 – Starbucks coffee house
March = 3   26 = 26   3+26 = **29** – Our special number

Des Moines, Washington, Saturday morning, March 27, 2004
Wanda and I decide to go out for breakfast before I report to work at my second job taking weather observations; she'll be heading down to her mothers in Olympia to spend the night.

The phone rings as I begin to walk down the stairs to the front door. I don't recognize the number listed on the caller ID. It's obvious to me that whoever it is, he is trying to disguise his voice.

"Who is this?" I ask. I'm ready to disconnect when the caller replies, "John."

"John?" I question, perplexed.

"Your nephew, John David," he says with a slight hint of sarcasm.

This was quite the surprise since John has never called. "What do I owe for this little treat on a Saturday morning?"

"I just called to let you know my Aunt Rita and her daughter are taking a picture of Mike to the photo shop for enlarging as we speak."

I warm with satisfaction. "Wow, that's cool," I remark. "I guess my little story at the funeral must've done some good. Do you know where they're going to put it at the church?"

"They don't know yet, but I'll let you know after the wedding," he offers.

We exchange pleasantries a few more minutes before I say, "Thanks for calling, John. Wanda and I will see you in July at Tim's wedding in Columbus."

3/27/2004

3= **3**   27= 2+7= **9**   2004 = **24**

3 positive numbers in theory

Renton tower, Monday morning, April 5, 2004
I have about thirty minutes before I have to officially open the tower; my inner senses tell me to check Suzane's web site. Once logged on, I go directly to her message board where the topic involves a seminar she conducted in Boston the previous Thursday night:

A lady expresses her experience as incredible. She was dying to ask Suzane a question regarding some numbers as a sign from a D.P. (Dead Person). Having asked about another subject earlier that evening that prompted a few chuckles and laughs, she decided not to ask the question.

On the way home from the seminar, she kicked herself for not having the courage to follow through with her thought impulse; nevertheless, she did have the good sense to pick up a copy of Suzane's latest book: **"everything happens for a reason."**

After returning home, she begins reading and soon discovers the answer to her unasked question while a calming sensation flows through her body. The chapter topic is communication; the paragraph topic is using numbers as a form of communication... **and the pages are 19/20.**

My story helps a stranger find the answer

Renton tower, Wednesday morning, April 14, 2004
I check my email before opening the tower at 7 a.m. In my Inbox is a letter from Suzane Northrop's assistant Linda. I'd emailed her March 31st to see if she could assist me in contacting another renowned medium's assistant; I needed help in obtaining a spot in

one of this medium's group sessions scheduled for Seattle on June 13th, 2004.

The group session was a last minute addition. I'd already purchased five tickets for John Holland's open seminar the day before on Saturday, June 12th with no indication a special event would be taking place the next day.

Linda's reply arrives about two weeks after my request. She's forwarding my letter to John Holland's assistant, Gretchen, and I reply back to thank her for the effort but the process is already underway.

Gretchen responded to my email on April 1, 2004: "There's one **possible** vacant seat left – the cost is \$175.00."

I quickly email a reply to Gretchen concerning my story and my urgency in being part of this group. "I can't stress the importance in obtaining one of these seats."

1-seat / \$175.00 / 2004

1= **1**   175= 1+7+5= 13 = 1+3 = **4**   2004= **24**

14/24

On my way home from work I stop by a drugstore when my cell phone rings around noon; it's Gretchen, John Holland's assistant.

"I just want to confirm your spot in John's group session," she says. "You're getting the **eighth** and **final seat**."

"Thanks. I really appreciate this."

I explained a little more about my situation and why I fervently sought to be a part of the session. After finishing, I provided Gretchen the financial information needed to secure my seat.

When I broached the question about getting John's approval to use his name in my book describing last year's seminar, she suggested I bring an excerpt copy for John's business manager Simon to look over.

"I won't mention anything to John about this," she confides. "The less he knows the better it is for you; besides, I doubt he'd even remember anything involving last year's seminar."

Wanda and I walk into the classroom at the Mountaineer's Club in downtown Seattle early one Saturday morning in June, 2003. The renowned medium John Holland will demonstrate his abilities and gift to an audience of approximately 150 people.

John takes a break to autograph books and CD's prior to the spiritual reading. Wanda and I are last in line, and when our turn comes I hand him my book and he begins to sign the front page.

I thank him for coming to Seattle and remark that his story was very interesting.

"The last medium we've seen is Suzane Northrop," I inform. "In fact, she wrote something about our situation in her latest book on pages 19 and 20 if you get a chance to read it."

*He drops the pen on the table; he slides his chair backwards as he raises his arm with his finger pointing directly at me. His eyes look intently at Wanda and I "**You're him!**" he declares in a loud voice.*

I let Gretchen know that Wanda and I, along with a few friends, will also be attending the seminar the previous day. At the mention of this, she became a little concerned.

"I hope you don't have a reading then," she states. "This would really make it harder on John at the group session; he might remember various items validated by you on Saturday."

I tell her I'm not only interested in receiving messages from my son, but I have many family and friends who've crossed over from whom I'm also interested in hearing.

"I'm open to the whole process," I admit. "If my son can't make it, I've got a lot of other people I'd like to help get their message out to this world."

She agrees. "We'll just let the Universe handle what's suppose to happen and not worry about it."

**2 messages from the office of World Class
Mediums on the same day**
4/14/2004
4+1+4 = **9**   2004 = **24**

9/24 - Sean's birth month and day
14/24

Renton tower, Thursday morning, April 15, 2004
I'm sitting on position, staring out the window and watching small, white, puffy cumulus clouds blowing across the skies in a northeasterly direction. Occasionally, a few are closely grouped together; I try to recognize the form of an animal most associated with the shape of the clouds. I've only talked with three airplanes in the past two hours.

Today marks the one-month anniversary of my mother's death. I still regret not making it back to Ohio before her passing. I kept putting off a trip to Cleveland because of our planned trip to Columbus the first week in July. I knew we'd be driving to Cleveland after the wedding and I'd see her at that time.

As thoughts of my mother swirl in my head like a western plains dust devil, my hands begin to jot down numbers. What I see confirms what I sensed as I sat in the front row at her memorial service: Sean was there to welcome his grandmother as she crossed over into her new life.

3/20/1920 - Mom's date of birth
3= **3**
20 & 1920 = 2+1+9+2 = **14**
1920 = 19 / 20
19+20 = 39 = **93** (reversed)
19 / 20 = pages in Suzane Northrop's book
3/15/2004 - Mom's date of death
3 & 15= 3+1+5 = **9**
2004= **24**
3/15/2004 = 3+1+5+2+4 = 15 = 1+5 = **6**
3/20/1920 = 3+2+1+9+2 = 17 = 1+7 = **8**
3/14/93 – date of death
9/24/68 – date of birth

I talked about my childhood friend Al earlier in my story. Through the help of a mutual childhood friend, who's now a corporate lawyer, I was successful in obtaining Al's address and contact information after thirty-five long years.

My first contact with him happens in September of 2003; this is thirty-five years after I last saw him in Willoughby, Ohio.

My ex-wife Pat and I attended a party at Al's parent's house in 1968; a party to honor our attorney friend mentioned above who had either graduated from or been accepted by the United States Naval Academy – or shall I say appointed by a United States Congressman. The details are a little fuzzy after all of these years.

Sean had another two to three months to go until his birth September 24, 1968 in Cleveland.

$$1968 - 2003 = \mathbf{35} \text{ years}$$
Sean & Al would've met spiritually at the party
September = 1968 - Sean's birth
September = 2003 - contact with Al
35 years = contact with Al / Sean's age in September 2003 if alive today

Des Moines, Washington, Tuesday night 1:30 a.m., April 27, 2004

It's been months since I last heard from Al. I've been a little worried about possibly coming on too strong with my spiritual beliefs and chasing him away for another thirty-five years.

The second or third email I received from Al brought me up to date on his past life/marriages/schooling and work history. It also held several keys that jumped off the page because of my heightened spiritual awareness; key such as his ex-wife and mother of his only son recently passing away in July, 2003. His son had just turned **fourteen** and Al's father had passed away in **1993.**

I feel a compulsion to get out of bed and attempt another email contact. I update him on current events in my life, and how these number occurrences seem to happen more and more as I get closer to an upcoming event. John Holland's seminar is less than two months away.

To this day I can't figure out why Al and his family's life are so important to my story. The numbers only show our interconnection; I have to allow time to reveal the reasons and meaning.

September 3, 2003 - first contact after 35 years
September 3 = (9)-September & 3 = **93**
3= March   93= Year   39= Sean's name alphabet placement
April 27, 2004 - this e-mail writing
April 27, 2004 = 27= 2+7= **9**   2004= **24**
9/24 - Sean's month & day of birth

Renton tower, Wednesday morning, April 28, 2004
I notice Marilynn's car in the parking lot as I approach the tower. She's been the lady in charge of cleaning our facility for the past several years; she's also been a major influence on certain events happening in my life regarding Sean.

Upon entering my second floor office I notice a large, plastic **Blue Butterfly** on a metal stake **lying on my desk**.

"Good morning, son," I acknowledge automatically before wondering why and how this butterfly got on my desk.

I stride up the remaining three flights of stairs to the tower cab where I find Marilynn hard at work as usual. "Did you put that butterfly on my desk?" I ask.

"Yes," she responds with a smile.

Knowing the answer, I still feel it doesn't hurt to validate. "Why?"

"Because of Sean," she replies assertively.

"Why?" I question once again.

Marilynn decides it's time to spell it out and let me know she's been paying attention in our class time discussions.

"A **Blue Butterfly** is what his mother sees **around his grave** each time she visits," she recites. "It's also like the **Blue Butterfly tattoo** you saw **at the coffee shop** last month."

"So what made you buy it?" I probe.

She talks about her shopping adventure over the weekend. "I saw it in one of the stores I was in," she says. "However, I didn't do anything about it at the time."

A couple of days later she found herself back in the same store. She saw the **Blue Butterfly** again and felt **compelled** to purchase it for me.

At this point I bring her up to date on my investigation of the butterfly after my coffee shop encounter.

"I never told you this before," I start, "but the date I talked to Sean's mother and found out about the butterfly was February 26th last year; the date I saw the tattoo last month at Starbucks is March 26th -- thirteen months to the day later."

It was almost time to open the tower, and I had to run downstairs to retrieve something out of my office. "I'll be right back," I said.

Upon my return, I noticed a funny look on Marilynn's face; she had something important to reveal.

"Remember I told you I came across the butterfly over the weekend?" she asks rhetorically.

"Yes," I reply with raised eyebrows, my curiosity starting to get the best of me.

"I didn't feel compelled to buy it until a couple of days later when I saw it again," she states.

"Okay," I reply slowly, trying to think ahead of her story.

"That was two days ago on Monday," she reveals. "Monday was also **the 26th!**"

It didn't take long after Marilynn left the building to put it all together. This in itself was a giant "**hello!**" from Sean. As Bill Cosby would say, "the proof is in the pudding."

February 26, 2003 – Pat's butterfly story
March 26, 2004 – Starbuck's tattoo butterfly
April 26, 2004 – Marilynn's butterfly purchase – **14** months later
Feb= 2   Mar= 3   Apr= 4
2+3+4= **9**
26= 2+6= 8 x 3 (3 months) = **24**
9/24 – Sean's month and day of birth
14 / 24

I reflect on all the times when occurrences or revelations occur during my times at the tower, as well as the many times when Marilynn is present or has been on site earlier in the day.

Her cleaning days are Monday, Wednesday and Friday morning. I've been trying to convince her that regarding the various psychic exchanges occurring between Sean and myself, she's a **high energy catalyst.**

My mind thinks back to Suzane Northrop's seminar on Friday, November 7, 2003. Wanda, I and a few friends (including Marilynn) attended the seminar together. I received a very powerful reading in regards to Sean and my number theory, as well as, a book promotion from the Spirit World.

I found Sean's and my story in Suzane's latest book while in the tower, as well as the reading I had with her in 2002 over the telephone. Besides all this, there has been the various emails and other minor revelations while using the computer, or while in conversation with people associated with this tower.

Last but not least, how can I forget Suzane's statement during our taping on "Northwest Afternoon" when she asked, "Do you know he likes hanging out at your airport a lot?"

Renton tower, Wednesday morning, May 3, 2004

Marilynn left about an hour ago. It's another slow day, and I open the paper to the **Wonderword Puzzle,** a novelty which always attracts my attention. I begin circling letters to match the words so I can read what today's answer will be. After I finish circling all of the words, I look at the word clues above the puzzle and try to guess the day's answer. The question at the top is: **So beautiful**? I begin to write the circled letters underneath the puzzle – the answer is **Butterfly.**

Glancing at the date next to the puzzle, I read May 3, 2004 and smile. "Good morning to you too, son," I say aloud.

May 3, 2004 = 5 (May) +3+2+4 = **14**

The Blue Butterfly Story = Feb (2) Mar (3) Apr (4) May (5)

2+3+4+5 = **14**

The Blue Butterfly Stories

2 #3 #4

March 2004 (13 months) April 2004 (14 months) May 2004 (15 months)

#2 + #3 + #4 = **9**

13 months + 14 months + 15 months = 42 (reversed) = **24**

9/24 – Sean's month and day of birth

14/24

Chapter Twenty
Pieces for My Puzzle

After months of editing and re-editing, I feel comfortable with the story and pick up a copy of *2004 Writer's Market* at the book store. I weigh my options of publishing companies interested in New Age Spirituality and try to gauge what each company is looking for in the hopes of fulfilling their requirements with our story.

Needless to say it's very hard when those first rejection letters arrive in the mail. You begin to doubt the salability of your story; and even your writing ability.

I remember Suzane Northrop's seminar in Seattle on November 7, 2003: "Why's he showing me a book?"

I keep this thought in the forward section of my brain as I continue to mail out *query letter after query letter.* If I believe completely in the existence of an afterlife, I have to believe in my son; I also have to believe he was showing Suzane a published book that night.

My job is to find that certain publisher or literary agent that's going to make our book a reality; one who believes and feels as strongly as I do regarding communication with spirits in the afterlife.

November 7, 2003
11/7/2003 = 1+1+7+2+3 = **14**

Renton Tower, Friday, May 14, 2004

I walk up into the tower cab around 6:30 a.m. Marilynn stops cleaning after a few minutes. The previous week I'd given her a copy of the book to read and asked for any comments or suggestions.

"I've only read the first forty-five pages," she begins. "I like it! In fact, I didn't want to put it down, but I needed to get some things done around the house."

She goes on to say that she and her husband Bob will be going up to their cabin over the weekend. "I plan to get a lot more reading done at this time."

Des Moines, later in the day

Because my Friday shift is again a short day, I arrive home around 11:00 a.m. I've got a good feeling flowing inside remembering Marilynn's critique a few hours earlier.

I turn on the television to watch John Edward's "Crossing Over" show which airs between eleven and noon. During the first intermission I realize I didn't check my email at work this morning, and I run down to the computer room at the bottom of the stairs.

There's only one email; a publishing company responding to my written correspondence with an email reply:

"Unfortunately, the content of your manuscript is not compatible with our current needs. We regret that we will not be able to publish it at this time."

"Oh well," I sigh. "Maybe John will have something to lift my spirits."

I proceed back up the stairs and sit back in my comfortable chair, facing out towards the now calm waters of the Puget Sound and continue watching the *Crossing Over* program.

After a few minutes pass, I can't stop rethinking about the dream I had the previous night:

I'm on a large horse farm. People are riding horses back and forth as we stroll through the barn. The dirt outside the stalls seems very dark in color; stable hands quickly clean it to hide any trace of manure left by those horses being led back to their stalls.

As I look around, I notice other horses already locked in their stalls facing forward, as if hoping for a carrot by a passerby, or maybe a simple caress and pat on the head.

Wanda is walking beside me, along with her mother Fran, the kids when they were much younger, other family members and Joe. Joe is Fran's husband of many years and Wanda's second step-father. He passed away in January of this year from Parkinson's and other age related complications.

A thought of possibly buying this property comes up and what we, as a family, would do with it; a similar thought arises as I remember our 8 3/4 acres mini-ranch we sold before leaving for Samoa. We had two Quarter horses and a pair of female Blank Angus cows for breeding that we had to sell prior to moving.

I count 17 stalls inside the huge barn. Surrounding the barn are many fenced pastures, with attached areas to the various stalls for showing.

Looking across the far side of the barn, I notice a large area that wasn't being used for anything. I picture a small reviewing area with a few bleachers for showing the horses, or possibly for displaying or selling various antiques. We'd be able to add a coffee bar and knick knack shop for customers if we went the antique route.

We begin talking about the prospects of pooling our money together to buy it. If we decide to buy the property, I'd want to renovate the pastures and old fencing so it looks like a very expensive Kentucky horse ranch.

"We could rent out a lot of the pasture space plus the extra rental costs if they wanted to include a stall," I suggest. "These stalls alone will rent for well over one hundred dollars or more apiece. That's $1700 dollars a month for the stalls alone."

I remember vividly seeing Joe. He's first lying on a couch off in the distance. He seems to be still in his late eighties as he was at his *recent passing. The next time I notice him, he's sitting next to me on another sofa talking about the farm and **his thoughts** on buying it together. He seems much younger during our discussion.*

17 stalls - $1,700.00
*7+7= **14***
1+1= 2
*__14 & 2= 14__ left to right/ **24** right to left*

I must've day-dreamed through the entire *Crossing Over* program. Collecting my senses, I'm just in time to hear John's customary closing comments, as well as a question from the studio audience.

A lady is asking about dreams, signs and their outward meaning. "How do we know who they come from?" she asks.

John explains the importance of dreams in our daily life, and why we should write down the experience and keep a record or journal.

"By doing this, you will eventually aid yourself in gathering conclusions," he relates. "You'll start to see parallels and possibly get the answers you're seeking rather than having to ask someone."

To illustrate, he gives the audience an analogy using an airplane flying overhead. "Your relative may not be the pilot flying the aircraft; nevertheless, he or she is still able to visit the cockpit."

I recall the dream I had about returning to American Samoa. At the end of that dream, I find myself on the outside of an aircraft looking in on the pilot.

John's airplane analogy
5/14/04 = 2 (**14's**)
5+1+4+4 = **14 & 14**

Renton Tower, Monday, May 17, 2004
I'm very anxious to get to the facility this morning to hear what Marilynn has to say about my manuscript. "I'm not going to bring up the book at all," I think to myself. "If Marilynn has got something to say, I'm sure she'll say it."

Once in the tower cab I go through my normal routine in preparation for my 7:00 a.m. official opening time.

"How was your weekend?" I ask Marilynn as I move from one computer to the next flipping on the on switches.

"Very relaxing," she conveys. "In fact, I finished the book."

"Oh really," I respond, trying to sound casual. "Do I dare ask your opinion?"

She goes on to say my writing abilities are very strong and powerful. "I really like the way you take the reader back in your thought recollections."

"Was it easy to follow along with the characters and the content of the story?" I ask, hoping for more positive feedback.

"It makes for a very easy read," she says. "At one point, however, I felt the story seemed to change directions about halfway through."

Unconsciously, my eyebrows raise and my skin wrinkles at the bridge of my nose. "What do you mean?"

"The story leads climaxes in the middle, but it seems to follow a different path after that," she confesses. "It's like events or situations are happening, and you remain in that subject area to describe it in greater detail."

I stop fidgeting with the computers and look at Marilynn. I calmly explain how the book is divided into two parts; the first part is my journey into the afterlife in search of Sean, while the second part is about **our journey together** to make the world believe **there is** life after death – how the need to **emphasize the communications** taking place between us is important in order to drive my point home.

"Did you notice this change take place once you got into Part Two?" I ask.

"I didn't pay attention to the chapter numbers," she confesses. "I just kept turning the pages."

After my explanation, it begins to make more sense to her why my writing would take such a noticeable turn and direction.

"Regardless, the story and your writing are fascinating," she praises. "I know you're going to find a publisher one of these days."

A particular publishing company I came across in the *Writer's Market* accepts email queries. The name of the company is *Red Wheel/Weiser Publishing.* "This will save a lot of time from mailing out and waiting for a response," I think.

I chart out their number placement in the alphabet to see how it stands against our number theory. The results indicate a favorable chance of receiving a positive response.

The email I receive the next day confirms my feelings. They want a proposal package mailed to their office for review. I gather the documents together and stop by the post office to mail it on May 18, 2004.

Red Wheel/Weiser
Red – 27   Wheel – 53   Weiser - 79
27= 2+7 = **9**   53 = 5+3 = **8**   79 = 7+9= 16= 1+6 = **7**
9+8+7= **24**
Book package mailed 5/18/2004
5+1+8= **14**   2004= **24**

Toward the end of the month I react to a friend's suggestion to develop a web site promoting my book.

"Even though your book isn't published yet, you'll still be increasing your web site ranking," he informs. The more I think about it, the more I like the idea. Not only will it be a web site promoting our story, it'll be a site dedicated to memories of Sean and other family and friends who've helped me on this spiritual journey.

I create the site on May 21, 2004, and the date turns out to be a very good omen. In fact, Sean has a few other surprises lying in wait for me during the site development process.

I decide on the domain name **Sean's-corner.com.** Typing the name into the appropriate form field, I receive immediate acceptance verification, but a few seconds later I read on the computer screen: Sean**39**s-corner.com. Congratulations!

"Thirty-nine? Are you trying to tell me something son?"

To finish the set-up process I need an email account name. I try various combinations revolving around **numbers or numbers man**. Each time the name is rejected. "Okay, son," I say aloud. "Let's try this one!"

I type in: **number14man**...accepted! Congratulations!

Web site developed – 5/21/2004
Sean39s-corner = **39**
5+2+1+2+4= **14**
14/39 = **3/14/93**

Des Moines, Washington, Saturday, May 22, 2004
Wanda's still in Olympia with her mother. I have to work the weekend, and I decide to take a little afternoon nap to rest up for my watch later this evening. After a few hours shuteye my eyes open and I realize I'd been given more pieces to my friend Al's story.

As described earlier, one of his initial emails mentions the passing of his ex-wife Paula during July, 2003. As a reminder, his Dad left this Earth during the same year as Sean in 1993. Al's son Toby is **fourteen** years old at the time of email.

Everything in his email fit perfectly with my numbers theory, except how his ex-wife fit into the whole picture; that and what this picture means to the two of us or our families.

During our senior year in high school in 1964, I attended Mentor High School while Al and Paula attended the neighboring school South High in Willoughby, Ohio.

It's a day before South High's Senior Prom. I'm at the school sitting in the outdoor bleachers, visiting with a few of my old grade school and junior high friends from Willoughby. I offer to take an old childhood girl friend named Sally to her senior prom on short notice.

We watch as the South High School band practices on their football field. Al is a drummer in the band and our mutual friend Ed is the drum major leading the band down the field.

I didn't know Al's girlfriend Paula at the time, and I have no recollection of talking with or even meeting her. Because she was Al's girlfriend she had to be around somewhere during this time, as well as the Senior Prom over the weekend.

Unbeknownst to us, the football field's name will change many years later to honor Al's late father for his long career of dedication and participation in the Willoughby school system's Athletic Department.

The following are revelations produced by my short nap. The numbers below show **how** using my number theory in conjunction with **South High School**, my friends and acquaintances have become interconnected through the years; unfortunately, the **why** is still elusive to this day.

I can only surmise how life and everything in this world seems to be interconnected in ways we won't understand until our own demise. This story and others discussed in this book are simply minute examples of how being interconnected has touched my life to make me **a believer** in a way I won't ever forget.

1964-All participants in the same town (Willoughby)
except for (**Sean)** and his mother (Pat)
1968- Four years after graduation
Last time I saw Alan – house party for Ed
Pat is there and pregnant with (**Sean)**
(**Sean)** is there in Spirit; he's born 3 months later
1968 = 1+9+6+8= **24**   8+6= **14**
1993- (**Sean)** & Al's father pass-away
1964 to1993= **29** years
2003 – Re-establish contact with Al in September
1968 to 2003= **35** years
1968 (Sep) to 2003 (Sep) = (**Sean)** is **35** if still alive
2003 – (**Paula)** dies
1964 to 2003= **39** years   **39** (**Sean's)** name in alphabet
39 = 3 (March)   93 (year) – (**Sean's)** death

March – (**Sean**) dies / July – (**Paula**) dies   March to July = **4** months

September – (**Sean's**) birthday / reconnect with Al   Jul to Sept = **2** months

2 months & 4 months = **24** – (**Sean's**) day of birth

1993 & 2003 – Death years

1964 to1993= **29** years   1964 to 2003= **39** years

29/39 = 29+3= **14**   39+2= **14**

39-29= **10** years difference

1968 to 2003 = **35** years to reconnect with Al

29= 2+9= 11=1+1= **2**   39= 3+9= 12= 1+2= **3**   10= 1+0= **1**   35= 3+5= **8**

2+3+1+8 = **14**

After the above revelations, I'm very happy to finally find Paula's connection to my number theory. I draft an email to Al the next day to share my discovery, even though I know it's confusing. To reiterate; **the numbers are for me** and I only share them for information purposes.

I also let him know about the upcoming John Holland seminar in mid-June and that contact from the other side seems to increase the closer such an event gets.

Unfortunately, I still haven't heard from Al in some time. Before pushing the **send** button I reread my letter to make sure everything sounds okay.   Suddenly I have the thought to call him with the information, as well as emailing him a hard copy. This will be the second phone call we've had together since the beginning in 2003.

It seems Al's business network had crashed! He lost all email and phone contacts he had stored, and the system is still very shaky the past few months. Some emails make it through, but others are lost on a daily basis.

After catching up on old information and my revelations about Paula, I decide to alleviate my apprehensions towards the end of our conversation.

"Do I scare you by coming on too strong in this new Spiritual belief?" I ask Al.

"Not at all," he assures. "I may not understand your number theory yet, but the more thought I give this, the more I seem to remember how **Paula believed** in this type of thing as well."

My face beaming, I can sense Paula and Sean around me. A single, bright ray of sunlight finds a way through the dark, gloomy, overcast clouds above.

After hanging up, I realized I forgot to ask Al if he remembers which year the football field at South High School was dedicated in his dad's name. I decide not to bother him any further for awhile, and call the school district on Monday morning for the answer.

———————

I have a page on our web site dedicated to the memory of all family and friends who've passed on. I've also added their names, and a small paragraph summarizing something I remember about each person, to the "In Loving Memory" pages I'll have at the end of my book. I make a point to add Paula's name to both pages.

Renton Tower, Monday morning, May 24, 2004
I spend the first hour of my morning at work talking with Marilynn. I shared with her my dilemma over the weekend involving Al, and my afternoon dream providing some of the missing puzzle pieces.

"I just want to open the door to his mind...just a little," I confess. "What if this subtle message is from Paula or his Dad?"

Marilynn recounts her weekend and a discussion with her husband. "I started to think about our talks last week and mention them to Bob," she shares.

"Is he still against all of this spirituality?" I ask, remembering his head shaking at the thought of Marilynn attending the John Edward Seminar.

"Actually, no!" she responds. "He's really starting to take an interest in it."

One of their conversations involved her ability to assess a problem confronting her on a certain project and to find a solution on her own. "I must get this from you because of the way you are," Marilynn says she related to Bob.

After my talk about trying to crack the door ajar in Al's mind, a realization is triggered in Marilynn's mind.

"I just came to understand this very second," she admits. "The thoughts that go through my mind when I'm tinkering around aren't a learned trait from Bob; they're actually thoughts coming from my dad."

"Really," I muse.

It's been a long time for Marilynn to even think about her dad's passing. A variety of things happened in their life together that left them estranged.

Because of my talks about Sean and other Spiritualism topics, she's been able to set aside some of her pent-up anger, frustration and denial.

"Your dad has a brand new life," I'd tell her. "He knows all too well he screwed up your life; unfortunately he can't change that. You have to deal with the present, and the possibility your dad is trying to contact you and let you know he's around and watching over you."

"My contact with Sean comes through numbers," I explain. "Maybe this is **your dad's way** of communicating with you."

She then shares a memory of her dad she's held for a long time:

"His name is John King, but he likes to be called Jack," she begins. "He refuses to use his birth name John. He worked for a contract company at the Boeing plant in Everett, Washington, when he was alive.

"A piece of machinery designed to make a certain airplane part was delivered to his company building one day; it was too large to fit through the assembly doors at its assigned building number. After studying the situation for a short time, he came up with a solution: he designed and rebuilt a new machine that could do the job and fit through the building door."

187

"Since your dad also goes by the name of Jack like my dad and brother, I'll just group the three of them together like a ***three of a kind poker hand*** when I go to *John Holland's* seminar next month."

This analogy will work well if a medium starts talking about card games, the number three, or anything remotely similar. My mindset quickly goes to these three people in my life; I can then listen for other clues and information to see exactly to whom the medium is referring.

Marilynn arrived early this morning and had completed most of her cleaning duties prior to my arrival, so she leaves the tower shortly after our conversation. I still have a few minutes before the tower's official opening time, and I remember I wanted to call South High School for the football field information.

Willoughby is three hours ahead of West Coast time, so it's only 9:45 in Ohio. Unfortunately, because of graduation ceremonies taking place this week, the Athletic Director is out of the office until tomorrow. I'm given his name and asked if I'd please call back in the morning.

Renton Tower, Tuesday morning, 6:45 a.m., May 25, 2004

I place the phone call to South High School and introduce myself to the Athletic Director. "Mr. Platcar, my name is Dennis Spalding and I'm calling from Seattle, Washington."

I explain to him that I'm writing a book and why I'm interested in learning the date that the football field was dedicated to Al's father.

Mr. Platcar admittedly is unsure where to find the information, but he does offer one other possible source. "I'm sure Alan's mother will be able to give you the information readily," he says.

After obtaining her number, I decide to wait until leaving the tower to make the phone call; I don't want any planes interrupting our conversation. Having recently lost my mother and knowing her mental state at the time, I'm not sure what I'm getting myself into. I know I'm not going to rely on Mr. Platcar's assessment of her fabulous memory retention.

Al's mother answers the phone quickly; I take a deep breath and try to remember the game plan I developed on my way home from work.

"Hello, Mrs. _____, my name is Dennis Spalding. You may not remember me, but I'm a childhood friend of Alan's."

Her response shocks me; it's like I never left the neighborhood over forty-six years ago. "On the contrary, Dennis, I remember you very well," she says warmly. "How are you doing?"

After a little small talk, she is anxious to know the reason for my call. "I've written a book, and I need the date the South High Football Field was dedicated to your husband."

"What kind of a book?" she inquires.

I go on to explain about the death of my son, as well as my interest in Spirituality that has taken a hold of my life these past several years. I also try to explain the job of a medium and the purpose of my story.

The pitch in her voice elevates slightly. I start to feel the ice is breaking beneath my feet; it's only a matter of time. "You're saying you can talk to God?" she asks.

"No!" I respond, shaking my head and cradling it in my right hand. "I can't do that...that's not what I'm saying."

"I'm really sorry about your son," she consoles. "But I really don't understand what this has to do with me?"

I try to explain the **"In Loving Memory"** page in my book, as well as the **web site memorial page**.

"I'd like your permission to add your husband's name to these lists," I request. "I'd use the football field dedication date, along with a few of my own memories of him after his name."

The whole topic of Spirituality is beginning to upset her. I never stopped to consider how difficult this type of belief will be on someone in their mid-eighties; someone who spent their whole life believing in organized religion's standards.

A normal person didn't openly admit to conversing with family and friends after they've taken their final breath on Earth.

"This is all beginning to scare me," she admits. "I don't want **my husband's name** associated with a book like this."

A second or so later she says good-bye and hangs up. I can only sit and stare out the back window. I say a silent prayer to Al's father.

"I'll honor your wife's wish; nevertheless, I'm not keeping your name and memories out of my prayers and thoughts. If you happen to stop by at any time with a message, or just to say hello, I'll make sure Al is brought up to date...I promise."

Chapter Twenty One
Dreams and Validations

Over the years I've come to the realization my night dreams and afternoon nap imaginings always seem stronger, more vivid and open my subconscious mind to a visit from a loved one, after I've had a period of meditation during the day.

These visits, however, don't always occur the same day or night. They may take place days after, or they may not happen at all. Nevertheless, from a review of my record keeping, these visits did take place after a period of meditation.

I don't find myself meditating on a daily basis as most self help books would have you do. I meditate when **my thought process** moves me in that direction.

Des Moines, Washington, Sunday night, May 30, 2004
It's been two-and-a-half-months since my mother passed away unexpectedly. Previous signs, as well as this visit, assure me Sean met his grandmother at the end of the tunnel in the next world. I

truly believe she wanted to stop by on this particular night to let me know she's doing okay.

The following is a dream I recorded immediately upon awakening the next morning:

I find myself in the attic of our detached garage where I lived as a child on Johnny Cake Ridge road in Willoughby, Ohio. The attic seems to be much larger and cleaner then it was when I was a kid.

A group of senior citizens are gathered off to one side around a table, trying to decide if they're going to accept Mom into their facility. The cost is $2000.

I'm trying to convince her not to worry about this added expense. "I can arrange my bills and overall debt; I'll manage and get the money," I assure her.

Mom never liked having anyone pay for her obligations when she was alive. If she couldn't afford it, she wouldn't get it. She'd rather spend her money helping her kids, no matter their age.

After the divorce from Dad, her children became her life. She found no interest in dating another man; she was happy being alone. Mom spent her time shuffling between her various families and grandchildren; that is, until it was too much of a liability to leave her at home by herself. She went to the nursing home reluctantly.

*We begin walking around the attic area. I believe my brother Jack is also with us at the time. Jack passed away from a massive heart attack at our nephew's wedding reception in May, 2002. Along with his other medical problems I believe his diabetes got the better of him; he loved his bag of **hidden** jelly beans.*

I glance out a side window and notice the round, concrete fishing pond in the yard below. My thoughts drift back to the first day my parents came to look at the property:

I'm about 3-4 years old. A yellow-black-white colored belt is on one side of the pool hanging into the water. I'm reaching for the belt and almost fall into the pond. My Dad pulls me away just in time and hands me to my Mom.

I then remember my Dad hacking away at this belt with something sharp before throwing it back in the woods. The pond is filled in with dirt soon after we move into the house.

As we continue strolling around the attic, I'm amazed at the many curio cabinets stuffed with valuable old knick-knacks. There are so many I couldn't even count. I do remember some pertaining to World War II.

The last thing I remember is helping Mom down the center flight of stairs to await the decision by the senior citizens.

Johnny Cake Ridge Rd or 84th Street
Mom's age at death - 84
*2 (4's) above = **24***
*May 30, 2004 = 5/30/2004 = 5+3+2+4 = **14***

I have tickets to attend a John Holland seminar during mid-June. As usual, activity from the afterlife usually increases the closer I get to one of these events.

Not only am I attending his seminar, I'm fortunate enough to obtain the last seat in his eight-person group session the next day on Sunday, June 13th.

Tuesday June 1, 2004
Marilynn reminds me about our talk the week before. "I'm sitting in the car about ready to leave the parking lot," she said. "A song about a sinking ship comes on the radio."

During World War II, her father, John (Jack) King, a member of the United States Navy, survives the sinking of his United States Escort Carrier he's aboard. This had been family knowledge all of her life.

A song about a sinking ship

The two of us believe this song is just another way her father has decided to let her know when his spiritual presence is around watching over her.

Renton Tower, Thursday morning, June 3, 2004

I'm in the tower cab preparing to open for the morning. Marilynn is busy cleaning. I call her attention to one of the computer screens to show her my new website: **www.sean39s-corner.com.**

"Have you had any visitors yet?" she asks.

"Last time I checked the count was two hundred and ninety," I reply. "Let's pull up my web host site on Yahoo and see where we're at today."

Thursday 6/3/2004

6=3= **9**   2004= **24**

Website hit total – **314**

3 - March

14 - day of death

314 – License plate match 314HNZ

After Marilynn leaves the tower a short while later, I'm gazing out the windows watching the light drizzle fall from the dark, overcast clouds above. Wanda and I will be driving up to Bellingham, Washington the next day to attend the Scottish Highlander games on Saturday.

One of my controllers, Dave, who's the main squeeze of my Clan Murray Commissioner, Kathy, will also join the festivities.

We all agree to meet on Friday afternoon to set up our Clan tent, and prepare everything for the early morning start of the Highlander Games the next day.

"Why don't **you join us** at the games?" I ask Sean aloud. "We never did this when you were alive; besides, you'd get to see me in a kilt and listen to the bag piping music."

Invitation offered to Sean

Friday June, 4th, 2004 the road to Bellingham.

I made our reservations a few months in advance at the Hampton Inn in Bellingham. Knowing we'd be on the road early, I requested an early check-in upon arrival.

Upon reading our room key I welcome Sean to Bellingham in my inner thoughts. Our room will be on the third floor; our room number is **three one four**.

Room Key – 314

Renton tower, Wednesday morning, June 9, 2004.

I spend a few minutes talking with Dave about the Highlander games over the weekend. As I'm leaving the tower cab to go downstairs to my office, he tells me something I find intriguing.

"Kathy told me to tell you 'to tell your son to stay out of her daughters dreams!'" he relates with a smile.

I back up one step on the staircase; my brow makes a furrow above my nose. "What are you talking about?" I question, placing the stack of paperwork I had in my hand on the upper stairwell concrete wall.

"Jada had a dream last night," he goes on to explain. "She woke up this morning talking about **Blue Butterflies**."

Jada is Kathy's young five-year-old daughter. According to Dave, she's never been around the two of them when discussions about Sean or anything involving my story have been going on. But Kathy has seen firsthand a visit from my son at a seminar conducted by Suzane Northrop during November of last year.

"Why's he telling me **numbers**?" Suzane asked at the seminar with a quizzical look across her face.

Blue Butterflies

Des Moines, Friday morning, June 11, 2004

I took today off from work so I can drive to Olympia to pick up Wanda's mother. We'll be attending *John Holland's seminar* tomorrow; unfortunately, I'll be going alone to the group session on Sunday.

195

Opening my eyes, I'm looking at the digital alarm clock on the night table. It's not only strange waking at this hour, rather than my normal 5 a.m. (**I don't want to go to work**) alarm notification; it's also rewarding because of the dream I've just had and the time on the clock.

The time is **7:07** a.m. I try to find a pencil and paper to quickly write down everything I can recall from my dream about *John Edward.*

I'm walking into a movie theatre, and we're sitting around in our seats talking. The next thing I know I'm sitting next to Travis. Everyone around us has a blanket wrapped around them, because the air conditioning seems to be on the freeze setting.

I notice Travis has two blankets draped over his legs. I try to take one; he argues at first, but reconsidering he finally relents out of pity for his dad. He also remembers I've got something of his locked away in my car.

Suddenly, I notice John Edward and his entourage making their way down the aisle to their reserved middle row seats closer to the stage. I look around to see if anyone else recognizes him.

I begin to realize their seating is different than ours. They appear to be in recliner chairs that connect to a row of normal movie theatre seats. Inexplicably, they start swinging around in their chairs. One minute they're facing in our direction, the next they're facing toward the stage area.

The next thing I know, I'm walking up the aisle to my seat, and I'm coming from the direction of the stage. By this time, John's alone in his seat. His entourage has left or possibly gone for refreshments.

I see him staring at me as I proceed up the aisle toward my seat; he's got a confused look on his face. I stop in the aisle adjacent to his seat, and look in his direction.

"Are you hearing messages?" I ask.

"Sean!" he responds with a smile.

"That's him," I agree.

I take the opportunity and sit next to him. I try to relay bits and pieces of our story, along with my idea to write a book. "Don't wave your hand around like that," he scolds.

"Sorry," I apologize. "I tend to get a little excited when I tell my story."

"I'm seeing a lot of money or gambling," he relates.

I stop him right there. "No," I said. "The numbers aren't about gambling; they're about my son contacting me, using the numbers for a reference."

I continue my story, relating my dilemma in finding a publisher and dealing with the rejection letters.

"It's really a good story," I confess. "It's a story that needs to be told."

He jumps up from his seat. "Let me go find, Allison," he says. At that point, he walks rapidly up the aisle toward the front of the theatre.

I return to my seat; Travis and the blankets are gone. Wanda is seated in the chair with a large crowd; they'd all been watching my conversation with John.

"He felt Sean's presence here," I said. "I knew he came with us."

The crowd seated around us erupts cheering and clapping as they overhear my chat with Wanda.

Sitting back in my seat, my mind is chanting, yes, yes, yes, over and over, as my hands clench into a fist with a movement similar to boxers touching gloves before a fight.

"Wow, John Edward finally knows about Sean and our story," I say to Wanda, a congratulatory grin spreading across my face.

Date 6/11/2004= 6+1+1+2+4= **14**
Time: 7: 07 a.m. = 7+7= **14**

Des Moines, Saturday morning, June 12th, 2004

I told my neighbor Richard we'd be leaving the house by 7:30 a.m. The seminar is at the Mountaineer's Club in downtown Seattle and starts at 9:00 a.m. I'm the type of person who arrives an hour early to avoid being one minute late.

A mutual friend of ours will be going as well. Kris used to work at Judson Park with Wanda and Richard, until a well needed divorce sent her packing out of town in the direction of Port Angeles, Washington, where her mother still lives.

She made plans to arrive in town a day early because of the long drive from Port Angeles. We weren't at home when she arrived, so she headed towards Richard's house two doors away.

The two of them went out early to get a bite to eat. They began sharing their problems and happenings in their lives; they also continued downing drink after drink after drink.

Before they realized it, the time had passed them by. Kris didn't want to wake us, so she accepted Richard's offer to sleep on the couch; however, the guilt feelings got the best of her and she called to say she'll be spending the night at Richard's house.

Out of kindness (as well as not wanting to be late), I give them an early morning courtesy wakeup call to ensure they will get to our house by 7:30 a.m. I'd already volunteered to chauffer this morning.

"Tell Wanda I **did** sleep on the couch," Kris said just before I hang up the phone.

"Sure she did," Wanda responds with a knowing smile; this won't be the end of the subject.

Everyone chats amiably as we head northbound on Interstate 5 toward Seattle. Needless to say, each person is silently wondering what the morning holds in store for them at the seminar; except Kris – she's still wondering what Wanda's thinking.

Richard's been a nervous wreck since Gail, the love of his life, passed away from cancer in October last year.

I've been trying my best to keep him afloat during his down times and to reassure him that my son was there to help Gail during her crossing; more important, the two of them are around him now. The numbers I had put together regarding Gail made that perfectly clear.

The closer we'd get to the date of the seminar, the more I tried to remind him that "The Spirit World won't make contact most times unless they're convinced you can handle it. Anything is possible. Besides, it may not be Gail who shows up."

Fran on the other hand, sat in the living room before leaving the house, trying to convince herself that nobody is going to show up for her. Not her mother or any of her three past husbands, which include Joe.

"Even though Joe just died in January, he still might stop by to let you know he's okay," I offer. "A simple 'hello' is always good."

I know Fran's negativity about receiving a reading comes from her fear of the unexpected; she'd rather not have to deal with a medium firing questions left and right at her, when it's much easier sitting back and watching it happen to other people in the room.

Kris, however, is anxious and hoping anyone connected in her life comes through. She just wants to experience a reading.

Wanda and I have been down this road many times; we're both aware a seminar offers no guarantees. Nevertheless, when my number theory provides a strong energy feeling and the juices begin to flow, I can't help feeling a sense of excitement the closer it comes to the seminar's start time.

Saturday 6/12/2004
6+1+2= 9   2004= 24
9/24

Mountaineer's Club, Seattle, 8:30 a.m.

After parking the car on the side street, we walk to the front entrance at the top of a small flight of stairs. Upon entering the lobby, I recognize a couple seated on a sofa outside the seminar room; I'd seen them at John Holland's seminar last year.

She came to the seminar in hopes of hearing from her three small children. They were all killed one day in an automobile accident. She'd been divorced and remarried.

We take a seat in the first two rows on one side of the room. There's about thirty minutes left before the event starts. Richard uses the time to settle his nerves, joining a crowd of smokers gathered outside the front doors underneath an awning.

I use the time to talk with John Holland's manager, Simon. I want someone with John's group to review my story excerpts involving last year's seminar, so I can get a signed release from him. I don't want to deal with any possible legal problems if and when my book is published.

"I'll also be attending the group session tomorrow," I tell Simon.

"Why don't you bring the excerpts with you tomorrow," Simon suggests. "We can talk a little about it before the group session starts."

———————

The format of the seminar is the same as last year. At the end of his talk, John conducts a book signing session before the actual readings take place.

Richard and I are talking as John gets ready to leave the stage. He picks up a copy of his latest book off a small table on the stage and heads in our direction.

"Here's **your** book," he says, handing me the copy as he walks towards the back of the room.

"Thanks." I automatically begin thinking for a reason for his kind gesture.

I show Wanda the book and explain what just happened. Walking to the end of the book signing line awaiting my turn, Simon joins me in line.

"Did you notice that he said, 'here's **your** book,' not, 'here's a copy of **my** book for you?'" he said.

"Yeah, I noticed that," I reply, simultaneously thinking something is going on upstairs in the Spirit side of town of which I'm not yet aware.

When I reach the table I hand John the book. "Could you please autograph this in memory of my son," I request, not offering him

Sean's name. At the same time, Simon is letting him know I'll be attending the group session on Sunday the following day.

"Maybe that's why I see so many people standing in line over your seating area," he remarks. "They're waiting till Sunday when I can talk to you one on one to get their messages through."

I open the book cover on the way back to my seat, reading this inscription: *"In Memory of your Son; & Blessings, John Holland."*

"I'm coming over to this section of the audience," John is saying, motioning in our direction. His head begins to shake slightly from side to side. "There's really a dark cloud over this area; there's been a lot of death in a short period of time."

He begins to pace in a half circle. "I'm getting an older male who's showing me an image that makes me think there's a military connection," he says. "They were in for a long time...at least four years."

I volunteer a validation, "I was in the Marine Corps for a four-year term," I respond.

"Was your father in the military?" he asks.

"Yes, during World War two," I reply. "I don't remember how many years he served."

"He's showing me a son or a stepson," John continues. "He wants to let you know he's there with him, and he's taking care of him."

Immediately I think of Sean, bracing myself for the possibility.

"This person is also telling me you need to get your leg wound checked out by a doctor," he relates.

A smile crosses my lips; I can't believe this has come up at the reading. I noticed a red sore, about the size of a quarter, on the back of my left calf the previous day. I thought it was probably an insect bite after working in the yard. I was tempted to seek medical help but decided to wait.

"Does that make any sense to you, please?" John asks.

"Yes," I respond. "I just noticed this on my leg yesterday."

At this point, I pull my trouser leg up a few inches to display the round, red sore in all its glory to John and those audience members sitting close by our section.

"How old was your son when he passed?" John asks.

"Twenty-four," I answer.

"Why would they show me autographs?" he questions. "Like somebody writing on a baseball cap or something similar, please."

All through the years as Travis grew up, he loved to save everything. When he was very young, we flew back to Ohio to visit my sister. He carried all of his valuables in this one particular tote bag.

Every night before going to bed, he'd hide the bag under their living room couch, so his cousins wouldn't get into his personal things.

My sister would watch him come down the stairs each morning and head straight for their couch in the living room. "Here comes **the bag man***," she'd say laughing.*

As the years passed, Travis's interests turned to collectibles. Any extra money went toward the purchase of baseball and football cards and various other sports related items. He also took up comic book collecting and anything else of potential future value; if it came with an autograph, he was interested.

"My son collects baseball autographs and other sports memorabilia," I offer as another validation.

"I'm being shown my reference symbol for blind," John continues. "He's also telling me at the present time he can see really well."

I think back to my Dad's eyesight before the doctors' diagnosed cancer. He lost most of his sight within a three month period. He could still see off to the sides, however, his forward vision was gone.

"That sounds like my father," I respond.

"Do you have an upcoming trip in the near future, please" John asks.

"We're going back to Ohio next month for a wedding," I reply.

"Good," he agrees. "With this whole dark cloud over this section, this trip needs to be taken by the **whole family**."

His focus turns in the direction of Wanda's mother, Fran. "I'm receiving messages from a male father figure Chuck or Charles," he says.

Fran can't believe he's talking to her; she quickly develops the common seminar disease of **mental amnesia**.

"Yes, darlin, I'm talking to you," John prompts, sensing her fidgeting in the chair. His raised arm and finger point in her direction. "Whoever this is, they're also showing me big blocks of ice as a reference."

I look back over my shoulder at Fran. I can tell she's trying to think; mostly though, she's quietly praying Wanda will step in to help her out.

Unfortunately for Fran, Wanda is also drawing a blank. It isn't from being nervous about the reading; it's her unawareness of the information being presented to her mother.

"C'mon, darlin, work with me," John coaxes. "There's a Las Vegas gambling connection, as well as a loss of a brother reference they're also telling me about."

I'm caught off guard when I hear Fran's voice validating the large blocks of ice, along with the other references John is telling her. I listen and watch how Wanda's mom begins to enjoy some of these past memories being brought to light.

Within minutes of Fran's reading, he turns his attention to Richard. I scribble notes as the reading continues and the references and validations are explained.

Richard seems to be holding back, or he's in a mild case of shock. I truly believe he didn't expect anyone to come through for him; similar to Fran's feeling after waking this morning.

Personally, I didn't feel any of these messages came from Gail, his one true love. Knowing how Richard is still grieving over her loss, she'll probably stay away until she's confident he can handle any message coming through from her.

Before we know it the seminar is over. John thanks the audience for coming. Gathering our belongings, we exit the room and decide to head down to the wharf area for a bite to eat and to review what everyone just experienced; everyone, that is, except Kris.

I'm already eagerly anticipating the group session tomorrow night.

"Eight people with three-and-a-half hours of readings," I think. "Some of you still have a chance to get through with a message or two."

"Here's your book," he says
*"...this trip needs to be taken by the **whole family**"*

Chapter Twenty Two

The Number Fourteen is Everywhere

Des Moines, Sunday morning, June 13, 2004

"Why don't the three of us go out to breakfast before Wanda drives you back to Olympia?" I suggest to Wanda and her mother. "I've got the group reading later this afternoon, so I'll be staying around here."

The group session is to be held at the Residence Inn, located at 800 Fairview Ave, at the corner of Valley St. in Seattle, Washington, from 5:30 p.m. until 8:30 p.m.

Before leaving the house, I pull out the sheet of paper I jotted some numbers on; I show them data I hope will bring a positive reading later in the day...

DATE: 6/13/2004
6+1+3 =10 = 1   2004 = 24   1 & 24 = 1-2-4
1-2-4 = **14/24**
ADDRESS: 800 = **8**
Fairview = 93 = 9+3= 12= 1+2 = **3**

$$Ave = 28 = 2+8 = 10 = \mathbf{1}$$
$$8+3+1 = 12 = 1+2 = \mathbf{3}$$
$$Valley = 77 = 7+7 = \mathbf{14}$$
$$St = S\text{-}19 \: / \: T\text{-}20 = 39 \: (\mathbf{93})$$
$$3/14/93$$

JOHN HOLLAND'S PREVIOUS SEMINAR & TODAY'S GROUP READING:

May 3, 2003 / June 13, 2004

437 days apart

$$4+3+7 = \mathbf{14}$$

Residence Inn, Seattle, Sunday afternoon, 4:00 p.m.

After parking my car below the hotel in their gated parking area, I check at the front desk to ask where the group session will be held. The clerk points in the direction of the second floor, off to my right, at the very top of the staircase.

I'm about an hour and a half early. Fixing myself a complimentary cup of coffee, I take a seat in the lobby area, which has a central view towards the top of the building and the adjoining floors and rooms above.

Off to my right is a large cascading waterfall that casts a warm feeling throughout my body. Watching carefully, I study each person passing through the lobby to see if they're one of the lucky eight people that will be participating in the reading.

About twenty minutes later, I notice a person on the second floor walking in the direction of the conference room. Pausing briefly, he does a double take in my direction.

"That sure looks like John," I think to myself.

He continues toward his destination and confirms my suspicions when he walks into the seminar room.

Moments later, I watch him exit the conference room and proceed back in the direction of his room. Again he pauses for a moment and stares down at me in the lobby; I wave and nod my head in acknowledgement.

"I thought that was you," he admits, pulling up his sleeve to glance at his watch.

"I'm always early," I reply. "It'll give me time to meditate."

He offers a good-bye wave and heads back towards his room to do the same.

His manager, Simon, comes down to the lobby about a half hour before the start of the session. He takes a seat in the chair next to the sofa I'm sitting on.

I hand him a copy of the excerpts from John's reading the previous year. "Here're the copies I told you about yesterday," I say. "Hopefully John can review them to see if he's got a problem with anything I've written before I get it published; but I don't want him to know about this until after the reading today."

Simon assures me John goes in cold to all of his readings. We begin talking about publishing companies and agents; specifically how difficult it will be to get my story read.

"This is a tough market at the present time with so many books on the subject," Simon notes. "But don't let that discourage you. Keep writing and keep sending out your material, even when you think it's hopeless."

The other participants begin arriving and start checking in with Simon. He informs everyone that one lady had to make an emergency visit to the hospital for a family member.

"She wants to get here about an hour late," he confesses. "I had to tell her that once the door closes, John doesn't like to be interrupted. So this group is now down to seven people."

I felt sorry for the lady having to miss this opportunity to receive messages from her family and friends; on the other hand, I felt happy for the rest of us because the playing field just increased in size for the good of our relatives trying to get through.

The chairs in the conference room are arranged in a circle when we walk in. Simon gives a few last minute instructions before leaving the room.

About five minutes later, John walks in. He's wearing a pair of jeans and a dark sweater. Sitting in the chair directly across from me, he takes off his shoes and sits cross-legged on the chair.

Before starting, he goes around the room to have everyone introduce themselves; he glances down at everyone's corresponding name on the attendance sheet his secretary provided, to get a good feel for each person, their name connection and where they're sitting.

I didn't have to say anything when the introduction ceremony reached my chair; he remembers me from the previous day, and adds a little humor to help relax everyone in the room.

"I already know, Dennis," he jokes. "I saw him earlier sitting in the lobby. I think he spent most of the day here."

In a group reading, the spirit communication doesn't always focus on one person. The entities are so close together, John jumps back and forth between the members in the group. He instructs everyone to listen to the validations being presented.

"Don't hesitate to give me an indication it could apply to you," he says. "I'll be able to decide who it's actually for."

I'm John's first target, along with the lady seated on my left, whose daughter is competing with Sean trying to get John's attention.

"I'm sensing a Mother and Father figure coming through," he says, looking in my direction. "The father is showing me his right leg. The sign he's showing me, tells me he either wore a brace, or he had **polio** in that leg, please."

I envision my father. He walked with a small, barely noticeable limp, a result of his right ankle bone and surrounding skin tissue being much smaller than the ankle on his left leg. When I was old enough to understand what this particular disease could do to the human body, I was very happy my Dad had only one leg affected.

"I can validate that," I reply.

"I'm getting a Jay-Oh name from him," he continues, leaning forward in his chair; he's trying his best to focus and listen for the complete name. "He's also telling me there's another Jay-Oh name with him; not like his father, rather a son or a brother to you, please."

My dad's name is John. His full name is John Wellington Spalding, although he always preferred to be called Jack. My older brother who passed away in May, 2002 also called himself Jack. His full name is John William Spalding.

"My dad and brother are both named John," I offer.

"Is this brother passed, please?" John asks.

"Yes," I reply.

John remembers Wanda from the previous day. A message comes through to acknowledge my previous wife, or the mother of my deceased son.

"They're talking about twins in the family," he mentions.

My thoughts go to my two younger siblings. Gary and Greg are un-identical twins born thirty minutes apart September 5, 1952. Greg is the one who helped find the missing number fourteen in my number theory.

I can see why Sean acknowledged his uncle during the seminar in Portland. Besides wanting to thank him for helping me find the missing number, Greg's birthday is also important.

$$September = 9$$
$$9+5 = \mathbf{14}$$

"I can validate that," I respond.

John maintains his concentration. Some of the validations are acknowledged by Terri, but most of them pertain to me.

The other group members are busy writing down the clues and information as they hear it. John recommends this courtesy to the group, so the person receiving a reading can concentrate on the messages being given.

"They're showing me a younger male energy," he reveals. "His passing is very fast."

"I can validate that," I agree.

209

"I can tell you've done this before; I like the way you answer," John comments. "Is this your son, please?"

"Yes," I reply.

"But he's not a son from your marriage now," he presses. "He's the biological son from your first marriage."

"That's correct," I said.

He pauses for a moment before proceeding, his brain deftly sorting the information he's being told and shown before verbalizing the message.

"He likes the dedication, or the memorial; but it has nothing to do with his grave stone," he states. "It could be something involving... **school**."

Sean and Terri's daughter seem to be talking at the same time, in John's mind, trying to reveal a similar message. Terri tries to say the message relates to her daughter's situation.

John lets her know this is a male energy speaking, but he also thanks her for letting him know the similarities as instructed at the beginning of our group session.

After I validate the message, he asks for an explanation. I tell him about the web site I created in my son's honor.

"He's telling me his passing was very fast," John relates. "I'm feeling an impact to my chest area, please."

I quickly concur. "Yes!"

"He wants you to know the accident was not his fault," he conveys. "I can't tell if he's showing me he's inside or outside the car; however, he's saying he was alone, or the only one who passed at that time."

John looks for some clarification. "Did he live with his birth mother at the time of his passing?"

I explain how he lived with her during his college days, but he moved away from Warrior, Alabama immediately after graduation to start corporate training in Miami, Florida.

Over the next hour and a half, the spirit source of the messages battle back and forth around the room with the others in attendance. I silently thank those that came this night to give me a message; I still listen closely to the information being offered up by John.

"Sean!" he states in a clear, positive voice.

I quickly validate, "That's my son's name."

"Finally," he sighs. "Almost two hours into this session and I'm finally given a proper name."

"I'm also hearing the name, Michelle," he reveals.

"That's my brother's daughter," I acknowledge.

"I'm hearing Greg or Craig," he admits.

I explain that Greg is my brother, and Michelle would be his daughter.

I remember back to the seminar in Portland, Oregon, where Suzane Northrop also came up with the same two similar sounding names.

There's been an ongoing mix-up with the ages of Terri's daughter, Ashley, and Sean. John seems to think Ashley is the oldest and Sean is around seventeen years old.

"Why would he be showing me the number twenty-four?" he asks.

"That was his age when he died." I answer.

The light comes on in John's head; he realizes his mistake in switching the ages of Ashley and Sean. Terri fills him in on a few more details about Ashley.

John looks back in my direction. "Your son is saying he's your first boy," he relates. "How he's your favorite and number one son."

I validate this with a smile.

"He's talking about someone being retired, however, they're still working and they can't, or won't, slow down," he states.

"I can agree with all of that," I admit.

I think about my retirement from the Federal Aviation Administration in July, 1997. I begin working with a private contractor, doing the same type of work three days later. I also started working a second job on my weekends off in August, 2003.

"He's telling me to tell you to slow down, you're working too much!" John warns. "He also wants you to get your leg checked out. Go see a doctor."

I laugh after hearing this two days in a row. "After this second warning, I guess I'll have to make an appointment tomorrow."

John counters. "What?" he questions. "You didn't believe me when I told you yesterday? I think that message came from your father. But now you're going to go make an appointment because your son said to."

When I show my leg to the Doctor the following day, he recommends taking a biopsy just in case. I mention I received two referrals to come and see him. He shoots me a confused look, until I explain the referrals came from my father and son.

His confused look quickly turns into a smile, realizing how family members seem to overly worry over a loved one and their medical treatment needs.

I wait for the right moment while he's looking at the sore on my leg. "By the way – they're both dead!"

"How'd they die?" he asks, not grasping the whole concept of my message.

After I tell him the how and the when, he finally realizes there's something missing in my story.

I lost out on a great Kodak moment. Before walking out the door, he turns to ask if they used his name. "Don't worry," I calmly reassure. "They only said 'doctor' this time."

"He's talking about a dedication of some type," John reveals. "It's not a photo album; but he's showing me something like a book, please."

I nod my head in agreement. I smile because Sean once again validates my writing. "I am writing a book," I validate. I take a quick moment to jot down the information on my pad.

John glances down toward the floor, but then looks back in my direction. "He's laughing," John says. "This is big time to him; he's strutting around like a proud peacock; he's very proud of this!"

The next message is about shoes and sneakers. My mind hits a blank wall and I pause in my response; Terri grabs on to this message rather quickly. Her daughter was very active in track at school.

Unfortunately, I completely forgot about my **seven pairs** *of purple sneakers lined up by the front stairs behind the couch. I found them at a Retail Outlet Store for Nike.*

They were size fifteen. The store had them marked down to $ **2.00 a pair.** *I guess the purple sneakers weren't selling. For feet as big as mine, I buy first and criticize second.*

I also forgot about Sean being in track at school. I remember his step-dad Rob telling me the story about his afternoon jog with Sean. "I can barely make it home towards the end, and he's running backwards to keep me company."

7 pairs x $ 2.00 = **14***.00*

Luckily, after a few more validations by Terri, the ball is back in my court. "He's saying something like, 'Big-Tee,'" John passes along.

"That's a reference to his brother," I validate. "His work associates use to refer to him by that title."

He then continues with many odds-and-end messages. He talks about Sean having short hair; not bald like yours truly. A reference about tattoos also comes up. I explain how his brother Travis has a few at present.

"Unfortunately, I think he's looking for one more," I reveal.

When the contact reference to his biological mother, Pat, surfaces, I explain to John and the group participants what the present situation is on that front – **no contact!**

"Be careful working around electricity!" John warns. "He's also talking again about a memorial. How can a memorial be ongoing?"

I explain about the book and the web site; the "*In Loving Memory*" page in both. "This is done for all of the family, friends and relatives that are in my heart and mind daily. Every time a new person dies I place their name on the web site so they're not forgotten."

"Your son wants to thank you for helping other people and parents besides himself," John acknowledges. "This memorial to him and the others makes him very happy."

I say a silent thank you of my own to Sean for the kind words. Once again the messages begin to scatter around the room like paper on a windy day. They come to rest on one individual for a short time, until they're unable to validate a certain message and somebody else steps up to the plate.

"I'm being shown an accordion?" John says.

I raise my hand. He looks in my direction. "I play an accordion. I had about five years of lessons when I was younger."

"That could be another validation from your Mom or Dad, as a way of letting you know it's them," he suggests.

The spiritual visitors in John's mind begin to depart the room. They know he can't maintain this heightened state of mental concentration much longer.

As John returns to a normal state of mind, he begins answering any questions the group might have in the short time remaining.

But before that takes place, he looks in my direction again and tells the rest of the group about the copy of his book he gave me yesterday.

"I felt **compelled** to come off the stage and hand it to you," he said. He also brought up the dark cloud hanging over Richard's head. "Keep an extra eye on him," he warns. "It's very sad. Please let him know in a good way, that it isn't his time to depart; he's got more work to accomplish, if you know what I mean?"

I knew exactly what he meant. "I will," I respond.

"His friend says she'll communicate with him when the timing is right," he adds. "Just keep working with him like you've been doing."

After everyone else asked their questions, I wanted to hear John's opinion on my **Butterfly Story**.

"That sounds like somebody is trying to **communicate** with you **through numbers**," he surmises.

He gets up from his seat to walk around the circle of chairs and thank everyone for coming to the group session. He pauses for a second while shaking my hand.

"Why do I get the distinct feeling I'll be seeing you again, or more of you?" he states.

"I don't know. But make sure you hold that thought." I didn't want to tell him I already had tickets for the Mystical Connections tour in November.

He tells Terri and I to stay a few extra minutes to compare *parallels* in the death of our two children, because of the way they relinquished time to one another during the readings.

Butterfly Story number confirmation

Sean died in a single car accident when his car crashed into a **concrete** freeway overpass. Ashley was auto racing at a track event when something caused her to spin out of control. Her head came outside the driver's window and smashed into the **concrete** retaining wall.

"Was your son on a high school swim team?" Terri asks.

"I was divorced during his high school years," I admit. "I also lived out of country. I knew he participated in swimming and diving at school, but I can't honestly remember if he was part of the school's swim team."

Terri relates a dream she had: He was a stranger from a high school swim team. He puts his arm around me to comfort me. "You don't know me," he consoles. "But your daughter will be alright."

Sean & Ashley parallel accidents

Dave, Kathy and Jada return from their vacation in Florida the last week of June, after visiting with her family. I see Dave the following Thursday, July 1.

He didn't bring me back a gift or souvenir from Florida, but to my surprise, he carried with him another special piece to my spiritual puzzle. Because Sean died in Miami, is Florida being used as our connector?

"I didn't get a chance to tell you last time, but Jada had a second dream the very next day," he begins.

"Oh, really," I reply. "More butterflies?"

"In a matter of speaking," he answers with a grin. **"Fourteen!"**

My mouth drops open; my eyes widen. "Get out of here!" I exclaim, a smile creeping across my lips.

"When she told me she saw a lot of butterflies in her dream again, I asked her how many there were?" he informs. "She didn't hesitate one second on telling me the number."

Once again he provides a joking message from Kathy. "That's two dreams in a row," he relates. "Any chance your son can find someone else's child to visit?"

"Tell her she should feel honored that he's around Jada and watching over her," I advise.

7/1/2004 = 7+1+2+4= **14**

14 Blue Butterflies

At this juncture in my story, I decide to do a little additional number computing with my **Blue Butterfly story.** I first add the amount of butterflies in each sighting or written account, in reference to the word search answer.

Each sighting had a single butterfly, except in Jada's dream. I used Pat's original sighting as the basis. The months included February, 2003, along with March, April, May and June, 2004, for a total of five months. Four months I had one butterfly sighting each; in June I had one sighting of fourteen.

Butterfly count = 4 months with 1 each = **4**

1 month with 14 = **14**

1month & **4** months = **14**
Butterfly individual count + months =
1+4+1+1+1+1+5= **14**

Sean chose to use Jada's dreams because of her mom's interaction in our story, as well as choosing Dave as his messenger because of our work affiliation. It's another innovative way to get a message to his father and whole family; a big hello from the next world.

The wedding trip to my nephew's wedding in Columbus, Ohio has been planned for almost a year. It's not very often you get to attend a ceremony on a millionaire/billionaire family estate.

Actually, this is one of three estates in the family name. Even though it's the smallest, it still has all the necessities one might need: an airfield, golf course, tennis court, pool, separate entertainment hall with stage, and a large array of exotic animals in large pastures throughout the grounds, including zebras and white buffalo, to name a few.

After Wanda's step-father died in January of this year, we decided it would be good to get her mother out of town as well.

I talked with my sister Diane to see if there's any problem bringing an extra person to the festivities. I also let her know about the good omen overshadowing her son's wedding.

"He's getting married July tenth, two thousand and four," I remind. "You know what that adds up to?"

Her response is the one I expected. "Good, grief!"

7/10/2004
7+1+2+4 = **14**

Seattle Tacoma International Airport, Wednesday night, July 7, 2004

The late night flight is scheduled to leave at 11:30 p.m. on Continental Air Lines. According to our reservation printout, our assigned seat numbers are Row 17 seats DEF.

We arrive at the airport ticket counter about 9:30 p.m. to check-in.

"We're on the non-stop to Cleveland with a connection to Columbus," I tell the three agents behind the counter.

The male agent looks at our reservation on the screen. "Any problems with changing your seats to an exit row?" he asks. "You look like your long legs could use the extra room?"

"That works for me," I say with a smile.

We make our way through security and finally reach the departure gate. I sit down and look at the tickets to check our new seating numbers.

I can only smile and thank the spirit world for the last minute changes. I also know we'll be well protected on this flight as my thoughts reflect back to the seminar with John Holland.

I wait for Wanda and her mother to return so I can reveal my latest discovery.

New airline seat numbers – row **14** seats – DEF
3 seats / row **14**
*"...this trip needs to be taken by...**the whole family!**"*
Welcome aboard Scan!

––––––––––––––––

The days and months continue to pass quickly. Every day my hopes are high an acceptance letter from a publisher or agent will soon arrive in the mail.

As I sift through the stack of bills, I notice a pre-addressed envelope in a familiar writing style. I didn't have to open the envelope to know what the enclosed contents said.

Thank you very much for giving us a chance to review your material, *MY SEARCH FOR THE AFTERLIFE*. However, this isn't the direction we're going in at this time, yada, yada, yada. The letter is signed by the representative of the Red Wheel/Weiser Publishing Company.

This makes me all the more determined to get our story published. I go right back to the *Writer's Market Guide* to find another list of five possible companies and start my query letters once again from the top.

Des Moines, Wednesday afternoon, August 4, 2004

My hopes are high as I drop the five query letters in the drive up postal drop box in Des Moines. I exit their driveway in the direction of the QFC Supermarket to pick up some pork chops for dinner.

As I approach the double sliding glass doors, my eyes catch sight of an old poster in one of the windows. The advertisement is outdated, but the message it provides my inner strength and resolve is very much up to date.

At a local town playhouse, on July 7, 2004 a play named *The Butterfly Effect* will be performed. Is this another quick hello from Sean? Or is this a sign that **our** book project is moving along according **to plan**.

July 7, 2004

July = 7 + 7 = **14**

2004 = **24**

The Butterfly Effect

Epilogue

My dream as a youngster growing up in northeastern Ohio on the shores of Lake Erie, was to become part of an Indian tribe of the Western Plains. I kept a mock Indian tepee, with all the paraphernalia having to do with this fantasy, set up in the closest of my upstairs bedroom.

Whoever wished to enter my sacred ground had to offer me the familiar greeting back then: "How!" This strictly enforced rule was also accompanied by the visitor raising their right hand upwards in the air as seen on the local western television programs.

Is it possible this boyhood role has gotten me here in my present situation with a firm belief in the afterlife? I guess anything, or should I say, I believe everything is possible if one doesn't close off his or her mind to the fact that there isn't an answer to everything. Sometimes you just have to let faith intervene and leave it at that.

The Sioux Indians held a strong belief in **Spirits** and **Visions.** High ranking tribal members would fast days at a time to help in receiving a powerful vision. A vision of **Thunder and Lightning** was a vision sought by various medicine men believing that it will help give them more power in their everyday life.

It's been documented that Chief Crazy Horse attained his status among the Sioux Indians because of a vision he saw. The Nez Perce tribe is known to spend hours in a sweat lodge to cleanse and heal their spirits in preparation for such a ritual.

Do I have some form of Indian heritage in me that I'm not aware of? I don't believe that's the case at all. I did, nevertheless, move out to the Pacific Northwest in the late seventies and marry a lady of Indian heritage belonging to the Confederated Tribe of Siletz Indians.

Maybe that move, and my ultimate marriage, help plant my roots into a more spiritual way of life: The ground I walk upon, the trees I see in my daily life or the cool breeze I feel on my body all reflect vibrations from these spiritual practices and teachings.

When I lost my son in that freak automobile accident in 1993, I began to realize there's more to life than the direction I was heading at the time. I eventually dropped all traditional beliefs an allowed my mind to open up and accept whatever was being offered from the Spirit World.

I'm very thankful to Sean for guiding my thoughts and directing me down the path I presently follow. I have no doubt our story will be published one day in hopes of helping others trapped in similar situations.

His clues and messages will continue to be a ray of sunlight in my life. I've promised him our writing will not stop after the publication of this story. Our next book together will be called, *MESSAGES FROM THE NEXT WORLD – His Signature.*

Our journey will continue for as long as it takes to reach into the heart, mind and soul of those who will listen. When I can reach out and touch the horizon; it's then I'll know I've finally reached my destination.

In Loving Memory

The journey to my destination has lasted many years. The reward I find at the end of this journey, besides receiving communication and validation from my son, is the knowledge of knowing that this journey continues each and every day of my life.

With my son around me as a guide and shining star, we'll journey forward together into the future. Our message is simple: open up your heart, mind and soul to the possibility, that what is – truly is!

This story is dedicated to the memories of those who were with me throughout my journey. They will continue to be with me now... and in the future.

Sean Christopher Spalding – without his help and guidance this story would never be told.

John (Jack) Wellington Spalding – my father; he worked hard all his life for his family, despite pitfalls and errors made along the way. I regret not being there for his final breath of life. Travis and I

will always remember your HO train display: "Stop…stop…stop…
stop…crash!"

Dorothy Celia Spalding (Johnson) – my mother, Sean's
grandmother. Her children always came first, to the very end. Her
special receipt for **oatmeal cookies** will live on through various
family members.

John (Jack) William Spalding – my brother; he seemed to be
always one step behind, but he was always there when I needed him.
Keep your teeth in, and save a seat at the pinochle table for me.

Rebecca (Flowers) Spalding – my sister-in-law, she was always
happy and cheerful; she hated when husband Jack joked around by
taking his teeth out to give the toothless old man smile.

Mike Flowers – brother of Rebecca (Becky). We played cards
together in my younger days. I helped **him** get a message through
to his wife Rita, about their daughter's wedding plans. Glad to be
of service, Mike!

Frederick & Eleanor Spalding – my grandfather and grandmother,
Sean's great grandparents. Grandpa loved March music and
Lawrence Welk. I can still see him in his favorite chair, his right
arm up perpendicular to the armrest, and his hand keeping time
with the music. Grandma always had time for a game of canasta
with the grandchildren.

William & Leela Johnson – my mother's mom and dad, my
grandparents, and Sean's great grandparents that he never met. I
never met my grandma, but I have her picture. My grandfather
never paid the $5 for my inside the park home run. Okay, my foot
missed second base and they called me out. How about $3.00?

William Nelson Spalding – my uncle Bill, he had a great tenor
voice, and he loved to show it upon request. He was our happiest
and most jovial uncle of all. I will always remember *Toodles the
cat*.

Mark Spalding – my cousin Jim's son. The geography between
us never brought us together. I can see him and Sean jogging the
streets in Heaven together.

Uncle Dick Hopkins – my Cousin Larry's dad; he loved his cigars.
Uncle Dick was a hard uncle to get to know. He became a vegetarian
after the war, and developed and patented Diversa Signs.

Inez Seon – Sean's grandmother; Pat's mother. From the island of Trinidad, she's a lady I respect. She treated me the same after the divorce. I'll remember her warm smile and Caribbean accent, as well as those great tasting island meals she prepared during my stay in Trinidad.

Ina Wilcox – Wanda's grandmother. She hated when I called her grandma. "My name is Ina – don't call me grandma." She also loved the casinos.

Ralph & Mildred Peoples – Wanda's grandmother. Farm, cattle, and a little confusion on my part about who's who in this family.

Joseph James Lorello – step father, married to Wanda's mother Fran. He loved to talk about WWII. He was a major in the Army and stationed in Europe; he also worked in the Forestry Department. He loved reading maps to know precisely where he was. I will thoroughly miss his quick grin and chuckle at off-color remarks and sounds, especially since I was the one creating most of the of-color remarks and sounds. We never did make it to the *topless bar* together as promised. My thoughts are with you always.

Bert Henry – Wanda's step father. He died 16 days before Travis was born. I loved his sayings and adages. Ruff exterior; super kind heart.

K. James Shriner – Wanda's father; he always wore suspenders when I saw him. I loved the fruit trees behind his house.

Aunt Grace & Uncle Harry – she always had the reddest lips and broadest smile. He reminded me of President Harry Truman.

Uncle Ralph & Aunt Mattie – my memories are vague as a child; I remember they lived in Tennessee.

Uncle Charles & Aunt Agnes -- I remember his bald head and large Cigar – he always had a story to tell. She reminded me of a movie star.

Uncle Clyde & Aunt Clara – I remember fond childhood memories down on the farm.

Aunt Edna & Aunt Alma – they were both teachers and principals. My Christmas Eve's as a child were always spent in Ashtabula, Ohio; this is where they lived and taught. We had a huge family gathering for dinner, music by the piano, and bags of gifts for all of the kids.

Aunt Joanne & Uncle Paul – she loved sports cars and German shepherds; he loved Aunt Joanne.

Uncle Al Wolpert – he was divorced from Aunt Joanne. He gave us the GREATEST gifts at Christmas.

Aunt Ruth – she lived in San Francisco. I remember one trip to the zoo when we were there.

Robert & Marion Swiney – my sister Diane and Bob's parents. I never met his dad; his mom was short and sweet. Bob's a non-believer. I'm waiting for his mom to come through and tell me what he whispered at her bedside before she crossed over. I'll convert him yet with her help.

Kathleen Swiney – Bob's sister. I met her once at Travis' graduation party back east before her death. Her husband had millions; her smile was worth a lot more.

Chris Warner – Wanda's friend. Always in my thoughts because of the impact he had on Wanda's life.

Shirley Stephens – a friend I met through Wanda. She had a crippling disease. Between the two of us we could make light of the situation and I could always make her laugh, even when her ex-husband left her in Ocean Shores with us and we wound up taking her home.

Frank Bateman – a fellow controller I worked with in American Samoa.

He loved cigars, and he also raised the best pineapples on the island. Frank always had his shirt open or off. He was very light footed on the dance floor. "I'll try to keep my grass cut just for you!"

Nathalie & Mick Cartwright – our friends from Australia. She liked the ponies (betting), and he liked the clubs (bars). They made us feel like family during our visit with their daughter Billie, and their granddaughter Marika. "I'll remember not to use the word *'fluff'* when in public in Australia."

Elizabeth (Lib) Mele – a true friend. She helped when I was down; she gave me a direction and purpose in life. My career loss is my career gained thanks to her. I'll make sure I file important letters better in the future.

Lori Depue – our neighbor's daughter. She helped her brother and mother on a paper route. I remember her shining face and bright smile at our front door on various occasions. "Thanks for the forgotten name refresher!"

Betty White – Wanda's friend from Judson Park. Betty stopped by Wanda's bedside one night after passing away to say: "Thank you for being my friend."

Gail Ochoa – our friend from Judson Park. She took my rent money each month in the nicest way. Her true love and friend, Richard, will need our prayers and support from time to time. I already know she'll be helping us out from the other side.

John (Jack) King – Marilynn's dad, and a *sunken ship* survivor during WWII. He was also an aircraft mechanic like my dad during the war. He made some mistakes on Earth, but he's doing a great job in Heaven reversing their impact.

Pvt. (PeeBrain) Mitchell – a friend from my military days in Trinidad. He had the happiest personality; he reminded me of a black Curly from the Three Stooges. Thanks for your visit in Portland.

Deanna Platoni – we met for a short time in 1980, and your life was taken by a stranger one week later! You made a vivid impression in my mind, because you've been in my thoughts since. My hope is to let your parents and son know your memory lives on. I thank you from the bottom of my heart for returning twenty-four years later to help set the record straight for both of us.

Charles Sheridan – a firefighter in Klamath Falls, Oregon. He flew *Tanker 61,* and died doing what he liked best; he and his aircraft went down together while fighting a large forest fire in the Pacific Northwest.

Paula Leo – my friend Al's ex-wife, and the mother to Al's son Toby. She was also Al's high school sweetheart. Thanks for the message in my sleep!

Bryan Paul Abercrombie – I met his parents at a seminar for John Edward. A military man, he stopped by one night at a seminar but I didn't recognize him. I'll do better next time.

Marie Gildea – mother of Dave Gildea, one of my employees at the tower. We met at her grandson's graduation party a few years earlier.

Frank S. Rodman – father of Scott, an Alaskan State Trooper. Frank lost his life in a plane crash off the coast of Alaska in 1974. Your son thinks about you always. I'll listen at the seminars for information about airplane crashes.

John R. North III – favorite uncle of Scott. Was a major in the USAF flying a B-47 that crashed on takeoff in 1966. You took a major piece of your nephew's heart when you left so suddenly.

Cliff & Agnes – my dad's war time friend. I remember several visits to Michigan where they lived. We played the neatest games with their kids in the basement.

Russ & Ann Weigle – our next door neighbors during the sixties. Twist party in their garage (parents only).

Antone Tarasawa – our friend Dorothy's son in American Samoa. I remember the nice dent he put in my car three days before the sale; I also remember his very outgoing personality.

Barry Townsend – the Jazzman. I can't forget Frenchie, his favorite dog.

Gail Reed -- Renton Airport Manager and a work associate.

Mildred (Millie) Crookston – Jo's adopted Mom. She came from a large family, and was a take charge kind of lady. She had a lot of foster kids.

Clara Ott – mother of Julie Bailey. We never met but I hope you enjoyed the flowers.

Jeff McCulloch – Matt's older brother. You brought Matt and me together to help your son; I'll be awaiting further input.

Jerry Thames – ex-tower manager in American Samoa. We had a great time together. If you hear any more about a strafing run taking place, I probably instigated that one as well.

Dennis Wilson – controller associated. We had more contact over the phone than in person.

Maggie Hall – nephew Kalib's grandmother. Had many good times at the family get togethers.

Sister of Ryan & Courtney – I met your brother in Portland; you met my son in Florida. You both shared the number 14.

Ashley Bergman – We met at a group session. You and Sean volleyed back and forth to get John's attention.

Elmer Hanson – pilot/flight instructor out of Renton airport. You'll be missed by the entire flying public. I'll assume you'll be giving flying lessons to the angels in heaven.

Harlan Reed --Wanda's friend, Dewey's dad. We talked once in his kitchen.

Dewey Reed – Harlan's son, and Kevin's friend. He did what he liked to do best – nothing. But he did serve his country in the Navy, and to that I give a big salute.

Owen Larson – Wanda's friend. I have no memories; I never met him.

Bob Ware – Wanda's friend. I have no memories; I never met him.

Stephen Parker – another friend of Wanda. He was a bus driver that lived down the road; I never met him.

Gary & Ann Eddy – Wanda's friends, and her girl friend Bonnie's brother and wife. I never got to meet them.

Pete – one of Wanda's uncles by marriage I never met.

The Spalding Family Tree list of relatives dating back to 1619 – if not for all of you, I'd never have been here to write this story.

Author's Biography

Dennis Spalding presently lives in Des Moines, Washington, a small city south of Seattle in the Pacific Northwest. A native of Cleveland, Ohio, he is 59 years old and has been happily married to wife Wanda for almost 27 years.

The Spalding's have one son together, Travis, the book cover illustrator for this work and a 1999 graduate of the Seattle Art Institute. Wanda has two daughters from a previous marriage, and Dennis had one son from his first marriage, Sean. Sean was tragically killed in an automobile accident in 1993, and is the subject of this book.

A Marine Corp veteran who served his country during the Viet Nam War era from 1964-68, the author's first duty station after basic training was in Trinidad, West Indies, where **voodoo** and **black magic** are a local belief and a way of life for some.

It was on this small Caribbean Seas island where Dennis met and later married his first wife, the mother of his deceased son. In 1967, the Marines chose to re-ploy the author once again on a seven-month Mediterranean Seas cruise with the Sixth Fleet. This cruise practiced amphibious assaults on a monthly basis, as well as periodic rest stops at various ports-of-call in Spain, France, Italy and Sicily. This deployment would be the deciding factor that kept the author from going to Viet Nam where numerous of his friends from boot camp and Trinidad had already lost their lives.

Following his military stint, the author spent seven years with United Air Lines as a Passenger Service Agent in Cleveland from 1968-1975. His first son was born September 24, 1968, a few months after his hire by United.

Because of the liberal airline benefits and travel discounts, he traveled extensively to various locations inside and outside of the United States at minimal cost. In 1975, one month before his scheduled layoff with the airlines, he became an air traffic controller for the United States government. Six years later, he was one of the 5,000 controllers who believed President Reagan 1981's exhortation, "You have twenty-four hours to return to work or you will be fired!" Unfortunately, 12,000 other controllers chose to turn a deaf ear to the proposed threat.

His government career lasted over twenty-one years, and took him to numerous airports throughout the Pacific Northwest, as well as a tiny island in the South Pacific called American Samoa.

This small emerald green, exotic island is located halfway between Hawaii and Australia. Its chief harbor and town, Pago Pago, is situated on the southern side of the island and protected by the mountainous terrain surrounding its perimeter.

A lush tropical forest covers the hilly and upland summits over two miles wide by seventeen miles long; the warm, blue waters of the South Pacific Ocean surround this…Island of the Sun…from all directions of the compass.

During his six years on the island, inspired by the late, great Robert Louis Stevenson who's buried on a hillside of a sister island in Western Samoa, he tries out his own writing ability for the first time.

The fictional story uses the concerns of the air traffic controllers and their outdated equipment which caused the uprising in the early eighties. The manuscript was entitled: *August Skies 1981.*

Sadly, it met mixed reviews at various publishing houses, needing rewrite after rewrite, because of the technical issues and terms involved in the story line. The manuscript sits on a shelf gathering dust until it can be readdressed at a later time in his life.

Nevertheless, he did experience a form of notoriety on the island, in regards to television, radio and newspaper coverage; unfortunately, it took place because of local criminal activity and the **unwelcome** confrontations at his place of residence a few blocks away from the islands prison and detention facility.

On the flip side of the coin, in addition to the above, he did **welcome** to his home a chief pilot who'd attend the various controller/ pilot meetings arranged on an irregular basis; this pilot, however, was on the FBI's ten most wanted criminal list for killing his wife in a horse riding activity insurance scam in the state of Michigan. A book by Robert Ludlow, *With Criminal Intent,* describes the story in detail.

This important news flash wouldn't become known until six months after his return to the United States at his next duty station when a copy of the Samoan newspaper arrives in the mail.

After two tours of duty on this tropical paradise, he's reassigned and reports to his new work location at the Klamath Falls, Oregon airport tower. During this seven year adventure, he became known as, *Mr. Halloween,* in a community of approximately 37,000 people, for a yearly display that would eventually encompass his front lawn, driveway, garage, side yard and parts of his back yard.

It took several years for his ingenuity and creativeness, towards this Haunted House display, to reach the size and proportions that it did at the time of his transfer to Washington State. In fact, during the final year, he was told an announcement was made at the local Catholic Church to make sure everyone went to see this amazing event. Mr. Spalding was quite surprised when the Father introduced himself and complimented his efforts.

The weekly display, during the Halloween season, was cost free to the attending public; however, Mr. Spalding did accept donations. These donations would go back into the coffer for the following year. His motto, "I'll keep making it bigger and better with each passing year."

Because of this community service, he received numerous write-ups in the local paper, along with radio and television coverage and interviews. Unfortunately, it's during this time in 1993 when he received word about the death of his first son.

After a move to the Seattle area in 1995, he later retired from the government in 1997 and went to work for a private contractor performing the same type of work. This allowed him to receive his government pension and continue working as an air traffic controller.

It was during this changeover period when the roots of his **Spiritual Journey**, hidden away in the abyss of his sub-conscious mind, began to surface upward into his daily, conscious life.

Several years later, he began to take pride in his Scottish heritage and became a member of Clan Murray, helping out at the various Clan gatherings around the Pacific Northwest area. He's quoted as saying, "...I love wearing my kilt!"

His interests all through life have always been focused around books dealing with: Native American Indians for their spiritual belief, life after death, occultism, witchcraft, exorcism, Zen and spirituality. It didn't take long after the death of his son for him to find the teachings of the renowned psychic, *Sylvia Browne* to his liking as well.

Her meditation techniques and dream recording suggestions were practiced on a regular basis for several years in hopes of hearing from his son. After a co-worker mentioned the name of a new medium on the rise, and his God given ability to communicate with the afterlife, his dedication to Sylvia's teachings alone began to falter.

The first time he saw the show, *Crossing Over with John Edward,* there'd be no turning back. He knew in his heart he found the road he must travel in order to find his son...**in the afterlife**.

This journey is recorded in his new book, *MY SEARCH FOR THE AFTERLIFE – A Trail of Clues.* This spiritual adventure continues in his second book, already in progress, *MESSAGES FROM THE NEXT WORLD – His Signature.*

Printed in the United States
32180LVS00005B/20

9 781420 850772